THE END OF THE RAINBOW

THE END OF THE RAINBOW

How Educating for Happiness (Not Money)
Would Transform Our Schools

Susan Engel

THE NEW PRESS

NEW YORK
LONDON

Requests for permission to reproduce selections from this book
should be mailed to: Permissions Department, The New Press,
120 Wall Street, 31st floor, New York, NY 10005.

Published in the United States by The New Press, New York, 2015
Distributed by Perseus Distribution

ISBN 978-1-59558-954-5 (hardcover)
ISBN 978-1-62097-016-4 (e-book)
CIP data available.

The New Press publishes books that promote and enrich public discussion and
understanding of the issues vital to our democracy and to a more equitable world.
These books are made possible by the enthusiasm of our readers; the support
of a committed group of donors, large and small; the collaboration of our many
partners in the independent media and the not-for-profit sector; booksellers, who
often hand-sell New Press books; librarians; and above all by our authors.

www.thenewpress.com

Composition by dix!
This book was set in Adobe Caslon

Printed in the United States of America

2   4   6   8   10   9   7   5   3

For Jake, Will, and Sam, now men

CONTENTS

Acknowledgments   xi

Prologue   1

One: The Money Trail   11

Two: How Money Impoverishes Education   39

Three: Rich or Poor, It's Good to Have Money   81

Four: How Happiness Enriches Schools   89

Five: A Blueprint for Well-Being   135

Six: What We Should Measure   171

Afterword   197

Notes   201

Index   209

ACKNOWLEDGMENTS

I thank Mike McPherson, Harry Brighouse, Bill Damon, Julia Juster, Marlene Sandstrom, and the students in my fall 2013 course, Childhood in Context. The conversations I had with these students, friends, and colleagues were of enormous help to me as I mulled things over.

I thank the Spencer Foundation for supporting my first foray into the question of measuring school outcomes.

I thank my editor, Marc Favreau. He has been a joy to work with.

I owe special thanks to my sister, Jenno Topping; my brother-in-law, Chris Moore; my niece, Maddie; and my nephews, Charlie and Ike. They provided me with the most loving, fun, and supportive writer's retreat anyone could wish for.

THE END OF THE RAINBOW

PROLOGUE

Happiness is the meaning and the purpose of
life, the whole aim and end of human existence.
—Aristotle

Happiness is the truth.

—Pharrell

Think of someone you know who is well educated. What makes
that person seem so to you? Every year I ask my college students
to play this game. And every year they mention the most interesting array of people: their grandmother, sixth-grade teacher,
coach, or dad. When I ask them to list the qualities that make
them name that particular person, they offer a fascinating list:
"She is interested in the world around her." "He is able to teach
himself anything." "She's an insatiable reader." "He seems to
know a lot about so many different kinds of things." "She can't
be fooled." "He's compassionate and wise." "He loves learning."
They never say, "He's a good speller," "She's excellent at solving
verbal math problems," or "He can parse the hell out of any sentence." And in twenty-five years of playing this game, no one
has ever answered by saying, "He's rich." Yet in the daily lives
of children, parents, teachers, and policy makers, the pursuit of

1

money, rather than enlightenment or well-being, seems to be the driving force behind education. You don't need to be a detective or a psychologist to figure this out. You just need to listen when people talk about schools.

One day I was lingering in the cafeteria of an elementary school and overheard a small group of third graders chatting as they ate lunch. There were five of them, and it was obvious they had spent a lot of time together. They were talking with their mouths full, and at various moments raucous giggles erupted at the table. But they were also covering some important ground. At first they were speculating on what had happened to a classmate who was missing from school that day. They came up with various possibilities (sickness, a trip, a broken foot, and playing hooky) and then suddenly changed direction, as eight-year-olds often do, and began discussing the tests they had to take at the end of the week. One of them said, "My mom keeps telling me I hafta concentrate, that I hafta do my best, or I'm gonna stay back next year." Another nodded, tomato sauce squishing out of both corners of her mouth, and said, "I know. Why do we? I don't even wanna go to college." One of them jumped in with, "You do. You oughta. You wanna be rich, don't you? I'm gonna be a millionaire."

But should the primary purpose of education be to ensure that people can make money? Shouldn't education aim for something deeper and more ennobling than wealth?

This book is about what we really want our children to get out of school. Though it may seem like an obvious and well-worn topic, people don't actually think it through too often or too carefully. I have spent the last thirty-five years talking with parents, researchers, and teachers, as well as children themselves, and I rarely hear anyone talk about the larger purposes of education. Perhaps that's because everyone implicitly assumes that they already know and that the answer is obvious. But it is not. Scratch a little below the surface and it quickly becomes clear that many of us are muddled about the aims of education, and that a probing conversation would reveal deep differences among us. One person will emphasize skills (kids should learn how to balance a checkbook, do geometry, spell, use a computer), another will identify certain essential bodies of information (children should know U.S. history, world geography, the Western canon), and still others focus on general abilities (children should become critical thinkers, astute consumers, good members of society). Many probably have no clear answer. Most parents I know waffle: some days all they want is for their children to love learning, while on others they feel distraught if a son or daughter has fallen behind in mathematics. Just as often, parents simply want their children to get through the day without a problem. As children make their way through grade school, meaningful educational goals give way to a much narrower set of concerns, concerns that revolve around money.

Years ago, I was in a coffee shop and overheard the following conversation between two fathers sitting at the table next to me. As I listened, it became clear they both had children in the sixth grade. One of the men said, with a downcast expression on his face, "Dan hates school. He drags his feet onto the bus every single day. He hates math. He says there's no point to it. He thinks English is boring. There isn't one part of the day he looks forward to."

The other guy scrunched up his face skeptically. "What's that got to do with anything? He doesn't need to like it. He just needs to do it. I mean, jeez, it's not a birthday party. They're going because they gotta be ready."

His friend tilted his head a little. "Ready? Ready for what?"

"Ready to make something of themselves. It's a snake pit out there. I don't know about you, but I want Rudy to have a leg up. And if he thinks I'm gonna pay for some fruity-tooty college, he's got another think coming. There's a reason for all this schooling. It's not just so he can feel good."

Nor is it just parents who think that education is first and foremost a path to a job. Many of our nation's most ardent advocates for education have made their case by showing that schooling pays off, both for individuals and for society.

When Bill de Blasio became mayor of New York City in January 2014, he quickly proposed making early childhood programs available to all children in the city. His concern reflected his progressive values and an understanding (long overdue on the part of politicians) that a good social and intellectual environment in early childhood is key to healthy development. As soon as de Blasio put forth his plan, he ran up against intense opposition. But what really stood out in the first days of this political conflict was how the newspapers covered the issue. The first articles describing de Blasio's proposal and the opposition to it said virtually nothing about actual children—what their daily lives were like with and without good care. Instead, the articles discussed the economic and political ramifications of the proposal—what might be gained in the long run if the city provided day care to its youngest inhabitants. Reading those accounts, you would never know anything about the real little boys and girls who were or were not eating, napping, being read to, playing freely in safe and pleasant places, getting their needs met by kind adults, and enjoying their days. Our somewhat single-minded focus on education as a means to a financial end, rather than on children themselves, evokes a much earlier time when children were viewed primarily in terms of their financial utility.

In 1729 Jonathan Swift proposed a solution to the terrible poverty plaguing Ireland, with the long and expressive title *A Modest Proposal for Preventing the Children of Poor People in Ireland from Being a Burden to Their Parents or Country, and for Making Them Beneficial to the Public*.[1] In it, Swift suggested that the people of

Ireland could kill two birds with one stone by eating their babies. That way, he argued, they would both have an endless source of food and cut down on the population of those needing to be fed. Moreover, he added, it would be good for the restaurant business.

His satire seems ludicrous. Who would eat their children? Who would sacrifice the well-being of children for the well-being of the adult community? Only a society that hates its young. On the face of it, such a view seems opposite to the one we hold in the United States at the dawn of the twenty-first century. We bubble over with concern about children. This can be seen in the abundance of child care information, educational products, clothing lines, healthy menu plans for children, and media featuring cute children and offering advice about how to be the best possible parent. We appear as if we are a society obsessed with children. But actions speak louder than words. And just like the adults mocked by Swift, adults in the United States today neglect the well-being of children, particularly other people's children.

We allow children to be served food that will make them sick, both at home and at school. We tolerate the fact that millions of children have no access to good day care. Employers force parents back to work soon after the birth of a child, preventing them from spending essential time at home with their new babies. Perhaps most paradoxically, our educational system forces many children to spend their days in crowded and unpleasant classrooms in unsafe school buildings, encountering boredom, constriction, harshness, and disregard. So Swift's satire is a bit more relevant than it might seem at first blush.

Disregard for children's daily well-being expresses itself in other less direct but no less potent ways. For example, we encourage our least qualified graduates to go into teaching and discourage our most qualified from doing so. Soon after I got my doctorate in developmental psychology, I applied for a job teaching second grade. The principal looked at my resume and asked, "Aren't you overqualified to teach little kids?" Many of my students at Williams College tell me that their relatives beg them not to become schoolteachers, because it would be a waste of a stellar education.

Taken together, all of these facts about the lives of young children suggest that we care little about the daily joys and sorrows of our youngest citizens. Public discourse about children is usually framed in terms of what will happen when they are adults, and those outcomes are usually framed in economic terms. But this long-term connection between early childhood and economic outcomes need not, and should not, preclude a concern for what young children actually feel, think, and do. Money in the future should not obscure well-being in the present.

Our tunnel-vision emphasis on the importance of money has led to another pernicious problem. It has fueled an insidious two-tiered vision of education, in which there is one kind of school for the needy and another kind for the masters of the universe. Often it is the rich who promote such a view, thinly disguised as concern for the poor. In 2010 I wrote an op-ed piece for a newspaper in which I argued that we should replace the ever-growing laundry list of skills and information we demand of our classrooms with a simpler, shorter list. I argued that children needed time to play, to think, and to talk. The reaction to the piece was overwhelming. Some readers loved my argument and others hated it. One of the most vehement responses came from a venture capitalist, someone who had contributed significant time and money to supporting a group of charter schools in the city where he lived. He ranted about me in his blog, and I discovered how angry he was when the Internet lit up with responses from teachers across the country who were gleeful that I had made this man so mad. When I wrote to him to correct some misinformation, he wrote back to tell me that while the kind of school I had in mind would be great for his three girls, it would never do for "these other kids"—poor kids, the ones he was trying to help.

Over the past hundred years we have, without exactly meaning to, stretched schools in two directions at once. On one hand, we have demanded with greater and greater urgency that our schools lift up the bottom sector of society, bringing our poorest children, those with the greatest social, emotional, and intellectual deficits, into the middle class. While we've tinkered with schools to make them ever more able to do this heavy lifting, we have also demanded that our students learn more and more skills at the upper level—not just the basics of reading and computation but also literary analysis, algebra, history, computer literacy, public speaking, a second language, and the scientific method. Some people have argued that we should shelve one of these purposes and concentrate on the other. Others have claimed that we need two kinds of schools—one for those at the bottom, who need lifting, and the other for those at the top, who need stretching. In both cases, we have been misguided.

By allowing the pursuit of money to guide our educational practices, we have miseducated everyone. We are so hell-bent on teaching disadvantaged children skills (both academic ones, such as reading, and social ones, such as obeying rules) that will lead to a job that we fail to teach them the pleasure of being part of a literate community, how to make their work meaningful, or how to draw strength from the group—skills that might offer them a satisfying life. Just as bad is that middle-class and privileged children are pushed to view every stage of their schooling as a platform for some future accomplishment ending in wealth. This deprives them of the chance to figure out what they really care about, how to think about complex topics with open minds, and how to find a sense of purpose in life.

But there is an alternative. Some of the most intractable problems in schools could be solved if we replaced money with a different goal, one that would be good for all children, both now and in their futures—the goal of well-being, or what some people know as happiness. As psychologists and philosophers have been pointing out for centuries, humans spend their lives seeking happiness. And most parents, deep down, want that for their children above all else. The capacity for real happiness (as opposed to transitory pleasures) is what separates us from other species and makes the gift of the human mind so precious. School should be a place where children feel joy, satisfaction, purpose, and a sense of human connection, and where they acquire the habits and skills that will enable them to lead happy lives as adults.

Ironically, happiness seems like a dangerous aspiration to many people. Not long ago, I gave a talk in small town on the East Coast. I was arguing that the first task of high school principals and teachers is to make their schools places teenagers would want to be. A senior attending the local school came up to me at the end of the talk and said, "Most of my friends spend all day waiting to be done, so they can leave. It makes no sense." He hesitated, then added with a wry smile, "Well, maybe it does. Maybe deep down a lot of people believe that if kids don't enjoy school very much, they'll be better prepared to be miserable later on in life." He's not far off. Mark Bauerlein, of Emory University, has argued that it is a mistake to worry too much about student engagement in high school.[2] He reasons, just as the high schooler I talked to had surmised, that since students will likely have to endure a great deal of boredom in adult life, we'd do better to prepare them for boredom than to try to make school interesting to them. It's a tempting thought experiment: why not work hard to help children and teenagers become really good at tolerating tedium, irrelevance, and frustration?

Our educational system, however unwittingly, has been guided by the premise that boredom in school is an acceptable price to pay for future success as a bored adult. This approach rarely works.

Far too many children in this country spend their energy warding off the tedium, frustration, and constriction of school. At worst they end up dropping out. At best they simply put their heads down and try to get through it unscathed; sometimes this means getting through school without being damaged, but just as often it means successfully resisting new ideas, new experiences, or any fundamental change in outlook. Even when it works, though, it's a poor solution. Research suggests that even when students can tolerate sixteen years of suppressing their needs in the interest of future wages, things don't turn out well. They become dissatisfied adults. Which of us hopes for that for our child?

Schools could be so much better if they pursued a different aim. To change direction, we need to begin by tracing the roots of our current predicament. Those roots can be found in events that took place 150 years ago.

ONE

The Money Trail

The year is 1848. The place is Slabtown, Pennsylvania. Imagine a boy of thirteen setting out each morning to walk to his job as a bobbin boy at a cotton factory. He makes his way through the dark streets of a gray industrial neighborhood of Pittsburgh with his father, who works at the same factory. The boy is short and undistinguished looking, with a wide lower jaw and a broad nose. Six days a week, like many other children his age, he heads not to school but to a factory. He earns $1.20 a day, and his family just gets by. He remembers those days like this: "It was a hard life. In the winter father and I had to rise and breakfast in the darkness, reach the factory before it was daylight, and, with a short interval for lunch, work till after dark. The hours hung heavily upon me and in the work itself I took no pleasure."[1]

But his story, like that of so many Americans, begins elsewhere. Andrew was born in Dunfermline, Scotland, where he lived with his parents, his sister, and his brother until he was twelve. As a little boy he spent most of his time helping out at home. He went to school for a mere two years, but not to learn a trade. He didn't go because he had to. He went because he could, and just for a brief time. School was for him, as it was for all children then, a luxury, indulged in when a family could manage it. And there he learned things he didn't need for work. He learned things he wanted to learn. He learned to spell, he learned to add and subtract, and he learned to recite.[2]

But young Andrew's education wasn't confined to the four walls of that school. His mother's family, the Morrisons, was an informed and literate bunch. They were also atheists.[3] His mother's brother objected to religion so much that he deliberately worked in his garden on Sundays, a blasphemy to many neighbors and to his father's side of the family. The Morrisons were also political activists, writers, and journalists. Like so many children both then and now, his relatives shaped Andrew as much as his teachers did. Like many Scots, though living in a poor community, he was a reader. Even as a little boy he read plays by Shakespeare and all kinds of poems, many of which he memorized, at the command of his uncle. He learned about the history of British royalty from that same uncle, describing the history lessons this way:

> He possessed an extraordinary gift of dealing with children and taught us many things. Among others I remember how he taught us British history by imagining each of the monarchs in a certain place upon the walls of the room performing the act for which he was well known. Thus for me King John sits to this day above the mantelpiece signing the Magna Charta, and Queen Victoria is on the back of the door with her children on her knee.[4]

Looking back on that part of his childhood, the boy, now grown, sums up his early education:

I could read, write and cipher, and had begun the study of algebra and of Latin. A letter written to my Uncle Lauder during
the voyage (To America), and since returned, shows that I was
then a better penman than now. I had wrestled with English
grammar, and knew as little of what it was designed to teach
as children usually do. I had read little except about Wallace,
Bruce and Burns; but knew many familiar pieces of poetry by
heart. I should add to this the fairy tales of childhood, and
especially the "Arabian Nights," by which I was carried into
the new world. I was in dreamland as I devoured those stories.[5]

If books offered Andrew a dreamland, real life did not. When
he was twelve, his family emigrated to the United States, settling
in a community of other Scotsmen in the Alleghany region of
Pennsylvania. It was then, when it was clear his father's wages
wouldn't be enough for the family, that Andrew went to work
in the cotton factory. But not for long. He soon left his job as
bobbin boy and got a job operating a steam engine that powered a
cotton factory. He hated that job too, though he would later recall
how much it meant to him to help provide for his family. Within
just a few years he stopped working the steam engine, getting
himself a job as messenger for a telegraph company. This is what
he said about the new job:

And that is how in 1850 I got my first real start in life. From
the dark cellar running a steam-engine at two dollars a week,
begrimed with coal dirt, without a trace of elevating influences
of life, I was lifted into paradise, yes, heaven, as it seemed to
me, with newspapers, pens, pencils, and sunshine about me.
There was scarcely a minute in which I could not learn something or find out how much there was to learn and how little
I knew. I felt that my foot was upon the ladder and that I was
bound to climb.[6]

A mere two years of school, many more years of hardship, immigration, and dull work. Where would all of it lead? In his case, astonishingly far. Lurking in the pages of the poems he read, his uncle's stories, the drudgery of the cotton factory, and the thrill of the telegraph office lay enough to catapult this boy forward into a life of extraordinarily good things: money, erudition, accomplishment, and social contribution. Andrew Carnegie would become the richest man in the country. More important, he would give 90 percent of his money away to libraries, universities, and social programs well before he died.

Somewhere along the way, as biographer David Nasaw says, Carnegie determined not only to make money but to become ever more cultivated: "to establish himself as a man of letters, as well known and respected for his writing and intellect as for his ability to make money."[7] And though his father's family was more conventional and less cultivated than his mother's family was, Carnegie himself thought his own habits of mind came from both sides of the family. He would later attribute his enormous success to the families of both his parents: "So it seems to me I come by my scribbling propensities by inheritance—from both sides, for the Carnegies were also readers and thinkers."[8]

The familiar moral of Carnegie's story is that school is not necessary in order to achieve great things, that anyone who works hard enough and has some native talent and ingenuity can make it big. And, of course, it's true that every now and then along comes the rare person who can bypass the usual steps in life yet achieve great heights unknown to the rest of us. That was true in 1848 and it's true today. But there's not much to be learned for the rest of us from telling the story that way.

Yes, Carnegie made loads of money. But there are lots of rich people in history whom we don't remember at all. What makes Carnegie stand out was what he did with his money. And that is a story about education we can learn from. His fervent and deeply held belief in the value of books, music, and scientific discovery permeated his life and shaped his legacy. His determination to provide many with the treasures of enlightenment defined him in much more interesting ways than his money did. Carnegie's love of learning cannot be traced to his meager two years in school. Perhaps his uncle and the rest of his mother's family gave him his love of books, his hunger for knowledge, and his profound respect for the power of ideas. But the real lesson Carnegie offers us has little to do with his own educational path. Instead, he offers us a chance to rethink what kind of education we should strive for.

Carnegie's is a wonderful story for a book about schools, because just as he arrived in this country, crossing the transom between two homelands, between poverty and wealth, and between boyhood and manhood, education in the United States also stood on a brink, poised between its rural, somewhat haphazard roots and its industrialized future. When Carnegie arrived in the United States, formal education was still to a great extent a privilege. It was an entitlement enjoyed by the rich and grabbed in bits and pieces by the poor. In that era schooling was not intended to prepare people for work. If you could go to school full time, or even some of the time, it could provide you with good things that transcended work—a knowledge of literature, the ability to make an argument, a sense of the past—and offered a portal to life beyond one's neighborhood. But by the time Carnegie's grandchildren went to school, a mere fifty years later, all of that had changed.

During the mid-nineteenth century, schools experienced two seismic shifts that set American education on its current path. As industry replaced farming and artisanal trades, schools expanded their reach and redefined their aims. Up until the mid-1800s, fewer than half the children in the United States attended public school in any regular way. Farm children attended only during the winter months, when they weren't needed to plant or harvest crops. Girls often skipped school altogether. Black and American Indian children were completely excluded from the educational system, and new immigrants were just as likely to find themselves on the outside of the school building. School clearly wasn't for everyone. And for many who worked, it seemed completely beside the point.

When the children of farmers and tradesmen did attend school, they could learn the things that would expand their horizons just a bit. Like Andrew Carnegie in Scotland, a child here could go to school for a few years, or for part of the year, and try to get some smattering of the knowledge and intellectual tools that would enrich his life outside of the classroom. School needn't prepare him for work; his father or a local tradesman could do that.

However, during the nineteenth century, labor left the fields and shops and headed for the factory. This meant fewer and fewer people were at home or in the neighborhood store. As work migrated farther and farther from home, the farm, the small workshop, and the village itself suddenly lost its grown-ups. The number of skilled adults available to teach children was significantly diminished. One result of this was that many poor children also went to work in the factories, partly because there was no one at home to watch them and partly because the families needed every penny they could earn.

At least some people knew that working in a factory was not the same as working on the family farm. In his 1906 book *The Bitter Cry of the Children*, John Spargo lamented what happened when children stopped working alongside their parents and worked instead in factories for people they did not know:

> Children have always worked, but it is only since the reign of the machine that their work has been synonymous with slavery. Under the old form of simple, domestic industry even the very young children were assigned their share of the work in

the family. But this form of child labor was a good and whole-
some thing. . . . There was a bond of interest between them
[parents and children]; a parental pride and interest on the
part of the father infinitely greater and more potent for good
than any commercial relation would have allowed. . . . But
with the coming of the machine all of this was changed. The
craftsman was supplanted by the tireless, soulless machine.
The child still worked, but in a great factory throbbing with
the vibration of swift, intricate machines. In place of parental
interest and affection there was the harsh pitiless authority of
an employer or his agent, looking, not at the child's well-being
and skill as an artificer, but to the supplying of a great, ever
widening market for cash gain.[9]

Spargo wasn't the only one appalled at the idea of children
becoming adults by way of experience in a factory. Most of the
concern, however, was not for how factory work would shape
children in the long run, but over how horrible their young lives
were. This was a time when philosophers, biologists, and psychologists had begun to explore how children's needs were different from adults'. As the general public gradually began to realize
that children needed and deserved to be treated differently, labor
laws were introduced to protect the youngest citizens from the
horrors described by Spargo. Ironically, the labor laws, intended
to improve the lives of children, complicated a growing social
problem. If children couldn't work at home alongside a neighbor
or a relative, and if working in factories was bad for them, where
were they to go? School became a solution to a widespread child
care dilemma.

As urban populations exploded, city schools began to burst
with new students. In 1905 the *New York Times* published an article describing its growing population of students as an "army of
600,000." It was one thing to educate small numbers of children

as a way of enhancing what they learned at home, at work, or in their neighborhood. It was another to teach vast numbers of young boys and girls, children who were not learning trades in their communities. And so we come to another turning point in the story of American education.

It wasn't just that the number of children going to school began to multiply. These city schools increasingly included in their midst East European Jews, Chinese, and Mexicans. Black migrant workers from the South, the first of millions that would follow, began filling the cities as well and sending their children to school. As more and more different faces filled the classrooms of American schools, ideas about the goals of education began to shift. Policy makers and principals turned to the idea that not all children should learn the same things. There was near unanimity that masses couldn't and shouldn't learn what the wealthy few had learned in olden days. The school that was right for Charles Eliot, the future president of Harvard University, or Henry and William James did not seem suitable for the many immigrants, working-class children, and students of color that were now flooding classrooms in New York, Boston, Pittsburgh, and Chicago.

Schools began to devise specific curricula and programs for each population, depending on what those in power thought was useful. In one vivid example, American Indian schoolchildren in Tuskegee, Oklahoma, were separated from white children and "civilized"—made to dress like white children, behave as white adults thought they should behave, and learn trades that the white community deemed useful, whether shoemaking, cooking, or metalworking. In photographs of the Tuskegee Normal and Industrial Institute, American Indian students are shown operating a small cotton gin and making furniture. In a photograph from the Carlisle Indian School in Pennsylvania, students can be seen repairing carriages.[10] Though many of these schools thought that they were giving certain children whatever they were assumed to lack at home or in their community, in fact such specialization often served to increase the distance between groups of children.

But it was not just American Indian or black children who were designated for such practical lessons at school. Increasingly, work, rather than enlightenment, became the organizing principle of education for all schools. One citizen was quoted in a March 27, 1901, *New York Times* article as saying, "The so-called 'fads' in our public schools are no fads at all . . . but progressive ideas to get the child to do something with his own hands. Society demands that the graduate of the public school shall be able to do as well as to think."[11] There was a sense that the proliferation of vocational schools created a path to the future. Another instructor, speaking on the same subject, said, "Manual training and technical schools have but just started in New York."

In 1908, a *Times* reporter described seven kinds of schools to meet the needs of children in New York City: schools for "making young sailors," "the parental school" (for truants requiring manual and agricultural training), schools "for the mentally defective," schools "for the incorrigibles," "deaf-mutes' schools," schools "to instruct the blind," and "the industrial schools."[12] Most significant were the industrial schools, which offered evening classes so that working children could enroll. These night schools were described in the following way: "Undoubtedly the most important feature of this school year will be the extension of instruction in industrial training. Ambitious plans involving the expenditure of thousands of dollars have been formulated with a view to remedying the alarming situation which has arisen of children from public schools entering upon their life's work with no better equipment than theoretical knowledge." The writer of this newspaper article captured an important trend in public views of schooling, not just in New York but across the country: teaching ideas and knowledge that would not directly prepare children for work would be a waste of resources and a misuse of public education.

In other words, schools in this country did not open their doors to the masses so that the masses could lead enlightened lives. When they opened their doors to more children from a wider range of backgrounds, schools became a tool of industry and a path to earning money. Nor did this initial marriage of industry and education change much during the twentieth century.

This brings us to one of the more paradoxical twists in the history of American education. Toward the end of the nineteenth century, when Andrew Carnegie was already a rich old man and schools in this country had already transformed themselves into a system geared toward training rather than educating children, progressive thinkers entered the educational fray. John Dewey, the most famous spokesperson for progressive ideas about education at the time, argued that school failed to connect to children's lives and that most children found school to be irrelevant to their deepest concerns and interests. He pointed out—correctly, as subsequent research has shown—that from birth children are eager to become part of their community, keen to emulate older people around them.[13] This meant, Dewey argued, that they are more motivated to learn when the subject matter seems related to the life of their community. He put forth a compelling new vision of schools in which children would acquire knowledge through what he called "occupations" (for instance, carpentry and sewing, two that were used in his University Elementary School, which later became the University of Chicago Laboratory School)— activities that connected children to their society and brought knowledge to life. His work led to a flurry of educational innovation in the early part of the twentieth century. People started new schools, putting his ideas into practice and sparking great enthusiasm for reinventing education.

Over the ensuing century, similar ideas have periodically taken hold. In the 1960s writers such as John Holt and Herb Kohl offered similar visions of school as a place where children would care about what they learn and where they would learn things that were meaningful to their lives. In the 1990s similar ideas once again took hold, and people talked about the importance of the "active learner" and the value of "project-based" learning. Educators realized that most children learned more when they did things (building, cooking, drawing, and tinkering) than they did when they simply absorbed information (studying lists of spelling words, memorizing multiplication tables, or reading about previous centuries). On the face of it, these iterations of Dewey's seminal view made sense.

However, over time educators who believed they were carrying on Dewey's tradition lost sight of his actual ideas. A close reading of his books *The School and Society* and *The Child and the Curriculum* shows that Dewey had in mind the kind of intellectual achievement and self-actualization proposed by another progressive thinker, Charles Eliot, famed president of Harvard University. Like Eliot, Dewey firmly believed that the purpose of school was to educate, not to train. The goal was to help students become knowledgeable and thoughtful, equipped to construct and evaluate ideas in a community of others who were equally knowledgeable and thoughtful.

However, two odd things happened to Dewey's ideas during this pivotal era. First, they were twisted to refer to what we now understand as "vocational training." Instead of using the making of a wooden table as an opportunity to teach a child about the history of industry, the origins of materials used in fabrication, or the structure of an economic system, educators saw the making of a wooden table as an opportunity to teach children carpentry. The second odd thing that happened to Dewey's ideas was more important and had an even worse impact on our educational system. Rather than using occupations as a way to bring all children, black or white, rich or poor, U.S.-born or immigrant, into the world of knowledge and ideas, educational reformers seized on Dewey to emphasize the importance of job training. The mistranslation of Dewey provided a new and, to many people, appealing narrative for educating children who appeared to be academically unpromising.

In the 1960s, when progressive education got its second wind, those in favor of the most lively and engaged classrooms often also advocated vocational programs, at least for some children. These enlightened educators were intent upon awakening students' minds, giving them a chance to pursue their interests and find personal meaning in the subjects they studied. To them, those aspirations went hand in hand with their conviction that not everyone should be pushed into an academic path, that not everyone was meant to be a reader and a thinker. What advocates of progressive education in the sixties did not explicitly say had been put clearly enough, sixty years before, when journalists, educators, and those in power argued that an academic education would be wasted on poor children and immigrants, those from "dirty streets," "unkempt houses," and "ignorant parents," and that such children would profit much more from a practical education in manual labor. Most progressive educators in the 1960s, and continuing into the present day, may not have even realized that in advocating vocational training they were promoting a two-tiered system.

And what has happened in the last fifty years? Have we outgrown the belief that the purpose of school is to learn a trade or become prepared to make money? Have we figured out how to make schools a place for everyone to become enlightened? The answer is no.

In one sense, we are more ambitious than ever. We attempt to educate more children in more subjects than our parents or grandparents did. No longer are the basic skills that Carnegie acquired in his two years of school enough. Go into any public school and listen to the administrators discuss their expectations: we want all children to be literate, to be numerate, to understand the uses of technology, to collaborate, to make healthy choices, to be comfortable at public speaking, to have a grasp of chemistry and biology, to think logically, and to write a good argument (and that is the short version of the list). That collection of goals sounds lofty and far-reaching; later I will argue that it is an impossible list. But it is also not as broad a set of goals as you might think. When you actually hear educators discuss the items on that list (or some version of it), money is lurking behind every phrase. "Students of the twenty-first century will need to be innovators to work in tomorrow's industries. They'll need a firm grasp of computer skills to get a job," some say. Others talk about the value of flexibility in tomorrow's economy: "These kids will probably change jobs at least seven times. They'll need to be quick on their feet and good at learning new content." Even goals such as getting along with others are cast in terms of success on the job: "Look around. The people who get hired are the ones who can work on a team. These kids need to learn how to collaborate." In other words, all of our ideas about what children should be learning are hitched to a sense that a good education can be measured by financial success and that the peril of a bad education is poverty. This emphasis has slowly chipped away the higher aspirations schools might have come to aim for, carving schools into institutions focused on purely utilitarian purposes.

This preoccupation may seem inevitable, given our fairly steady commitment to the idea that every child should go to school. Native-born or immigrant, English speakers or not, intellectually swift or slow—the student body in the United States is more diverse than in any other country. The idea of universal education is as American as apple pie. Or perhaps it would be more accurate to say it's as American as McDonald's, since—as with food—when we think of making education available to everyone, we also think its quality must go down. To a great extent, the more we have defined school as the right of every child, the more we have conceived of that right as primarily financial in nature. When it comes to the individual child, school has become a path to economic security. When it comes to society as a whole, school has become the mechanism for eradicating poverty. Casting schools in terms of their impact on wealth and poverty has inexorably led us to treat economic success as the measure of educational success.

Evidence of this is everywhere. Several years ago, curious about the claims of several charter schools, I began to look for verification that they were doing a better job of teaching children than the standard public schools. I examined more than a hundred studies. The findings, which I'll discuss in a later chapter, were only part of the story. Just as interesting were the measures the researchers used. Some studies looked for signs that children who went to charter schools did better on specific tests. Others looked for signs that children who went to charter schools were more likely to attend high school and/or college. But all of the studies rested on the same assumption: that better results, be they in test scores or graduation rates, were linked to higher earning power once children become adults. Try as I might, I couldn't find any studies that didn't depend, either explicitly or implicitly, on a measure of financial security.

Using schools as a vehicle for advancing material goals has its roots in another line of U.S. history as well. On October 4, 1957, the Soviet Union launched Sputnik, the first satellite to orbit the earth. People all over the globe could see it, and its radio pulses were detectable. It was a dramatic and concrete sign that Russia was at the forefront of scientific innovation. It sparked what we now consider the Space Age. We were locked in a cold war with Russia, sure that we had to outperform them on all dimensions, and Sputnik was a catalyst for huge technological, scientific, and military advances.

Sputnik also launched an urgent discussion among educational policy makers and administrators in the United States. Up until the 1900s, science was not part of most children's education. Only the most privileged students learned anything about chemistry, biology, or the scientific method itself. Even for those privileged few, science was typically available only once they were in college. But in the nineteenth century intellectual luminaries such as Thomas Huxley, Herbert Spencer, Michael Faraday, and Charles Eliot began to argue that the study of science would teach children how to reason deductively, and that therefore it should be considered an essential foundation, not just for a few but for many. In 1916 John Dewey argued that science gave individuals the power to act independently: "Whatever natural science may be for the specialist, for educational purposes it is knowledge of the conditions of human action."[14] Within roughly fifty years, science had made its way into the public K–12 classroom. But if science education in its early days had been a means to a deeper, more rigorous understanding of the natural world and human actions within that world, in the wake of Sputnik science took a turn in another direction. Falling behind Russia in the race to space was a clear signal to our politicians, if not our teachers and scientists, that the existing approach was not working adequately. Science education was now seen as a crucial pathway to economic and military strength.

This urgent sense that education was a means for furthering national interests only intensified in the subsequent decades. In 1983, during Ronald Reagan's administration, the Department of Education published a report entitled *A Nation at Risk*. It announced:

Our once unchallenged preeminence in commerce, industry, science, and technological innovation is being overtaken by competitors throughout the world. This report is concerned with only one of the many causes and dimensions of the problem, but it is the one that undergirds American prosperity, security, and civility. We report to the American people that while we can take justifiable pride in what our schools and colleges have historically accomplished and contributed to the United States and the well-being of its people, the educational foundations of our society are presently being eroded by a rising tide of mediocrity that threatens our very future as a Nation and a people. What was unimaginable a generation ago has begun to occur—others are matching and surpassing our educational attainment.[15]

The report drives home the idea that failing schools would put the nation at an economic disadvantage:

History is not kind to idlers. The time is long past when American's destiny was assured simply by an abundance of natural resources and inexhaustible human enthusiasm, and by our relative isolation from the malignant problems of older civilizations. The world is indeed one global village. We live among determined, well-educated, and strongly motivated competitors. We compete with them for international standing and markets, not only with products but also with the ideas of our laboratories and neighborhood workshops. America's position in the world may once have been reasonably secure with only a few exceptionally well-trained men and women. It is no longer.

The risk is not only that the Japanese make automobiles more efficiently than Americans and have government subsidies for development and export. It is not just that the South Koreans recently built the world's most efficient steel mill, or that American machine tools, once the pride of the world, are being displaced by German products. It is also that these developments signify a redistribution of trained capability throughout the globe. Knowledge, learning, information, and skilled intelligence are the new raw materials of international commerce and are today spreading throughout the world as vigorously as miracle drugs, synthetic fertilizers, and blue jeans did earlier. If only to keep and improve on the slim competitive edge we still retain in world markets, we must dedicate ourselves to the reform of our educational system for the benefit of all—old and young alike, affluent and poor, majority and minority. Learning is the indispensable investment required for success in the "information age" we are entering.

Between 1848, when Andrew Carnegie arrived in Pennsylvania, and 1983, when *A Nation at Risk* was published, schools had made a 180-degree turn. No longer a privilege and a respite from work, formal education had become a necessity, considered essential to individual success. What had once been a luxury for those who could afford enlightenment was, by the second half of the twentieth century, a requirement for anyone who hoped to get a job and earn a decent wage. Schools were no longer a path to cultivation and a life of the mind; they were a path to a job. And that was just in terms of the individual. Along the way, as schools became a training ground for corps of workers, they also became a means of furthering national interests. The debate about schools had become part of the debate about national power. Which brings us to the twenty-first century.

When George W. Bush announced No Child Left Behind (NCLB), his purported intention was to encourage a set of practices and institute a set of assessments that would ensure every child got the same good start at school. Implicit in that formulation was the now familiar premise that it was up to schools to close the income gap between the rich and the poor. In its most beneficent form, it could have made a powerful difference in the lives of many children. If NCLB had ensured that all kids would learn how to read and that no child would become disenchanted enough to drop out, it might have been wonderful. But that's not how NCLB played out.

Within just a few years, teachers were rushing to make sure that each child got a higher score on the standardized tests than he or she had gotten the year before. School superintendents also felt compelled to see to it that their schools got higher scores every year. What had been promoted as a means of ensuring that all children received the fruits of our educational system became a relentless push toward improved test scores. With each year, more and more focus was on the scores themselves and less on the education the scores were intended to measure. At the national level, politicians threatened that if we didn't educate everyone, once again our country might fall behind. The conversation was less about giving everyone access to reading, thoughtful engagement in civic life, or the pleasures of ideas, and much more about seeing to it that everyone could earn a decent wage.

Nor did that focus change much when Bush finally left office. In 2008 Barack Obama replaced George Bush in the White House and named Arne Duncan secretary of education. Many people interested in schools assumed that Obama and Duncan would shrink or dissolve NCLB, which seemed to cause only problems for parents, teachers, and administrators, not to mention for children. But it has not been as simple as that. Once again money, albeit in a slightly disguised form, has shaped the conversation about what children should learn and why they should learn it.

The first thing Duncan did as secretary of education was to announce a new name for our educational agenda. Instead of leaving no child behind, we would now be in a race to the top. This meant, of course, that the United States would be racing to beat out other nations. It also meant that each child would be racing to overcome other students, getting to the finish line first. These twin motives are now embedded in almost all of the public discussion of education. When national averages of test scores are reported, they are typically presented as a table or graph in which our scores are compared to the scores of other nations. In 2009 we ranked lower on the Program for International Student Assessment than, say, China (represented by Shanghai), Finland, and Estonia but higher than Latvia, Thailand, and Panama. Yet, other than feeling this is a competition, it's quite hard to know what, if anything to make of such comparisons. In the end they tell us next to nothing about the children we are trying to educate or how our educational system is (or is not) shaping them.

But the national race is only one piece of the story. Take a moment to think about what it means to frame education as a race to the top. At the simplest level, it means that someone is going to have to be at the bottom. A quick look at the way assessments are currently done in this country shows the very real consequences this has for the lives of children. Children don't simply show that they can read, add, solve word problems, or interpret data. They must do better than other children, and better than they did the year before. Teachers, too, are rated in terms of this seemingly endless competition. Some have argued that it is good for everyone to see that education is a process, that there is always more to be learned, explored, or mastered. All of that sounds nice. But it's not the way children (or teachers) experience the race to the top. They experience it, for the most part, as a daunting and relentless grind. It pushes children to believe that success comes only when they can outperform others and their own previous performance.

An ironic symptom of this orientation is that teachers commonly talk of aiming for low scores one year so that they can show improvement in the next. The implicit belief that education rests on doing better than someone else is just one more way that a money mind-set has come to shape our thoughts about schooling.

When it comes to material goods, economists have a term for this worldview: they call it positional wealth. Just as you might expect, it means that you base your sense of how rich you are on whether you are better off than the guy next door. An example will show how ubiquitous such a view has become. I spend August in the village of Sagaponack, New York, where I grew up. Though once a farm community, it is now notorious as a summer playground of the rich and famous. When I was a little girl, the men I knew drove pickup trucks and the women drove station wagons. One notable summer resident drove a green Jaguar; everyone talked about it. As the summer population rose over the years, so did the standard of cars you'd see on the road. By the time my children were born, the summer residents had taken over the island. Now Audis and Jeeps were everywhere, at least in July and August. By the time my children were teenagers, the roads were lined with Porsches and souped-up Land Rovers. Every decade brought a new level of car ostentation. But it wasn't just the summer residents. Each decade the local population seemed to up their car game as well. The last time I visited, there was a Range Rover in every year-round resident's driveway. If all your neighbors have a Jeep, it's no longer enough for you to have one too; you need something just a little fancier. That is what economists means by positional wealth.

Now this principle is at play in the way we think about educational standards. It's not enough to make sure that all children can read. They must read better, whatever that means, than children in other nations. It's not adequate for a group of students to spell 70 percent of the words correctly. They must get a score that is 15 percent better than the students in schools one town over. I have watched the local community react when test scores are printed in our community newspaper. The first thing people talk about is which schools did better than the others and which did worse. Schools that were doing fine all along (that is, where most kids could read a page of text by the time they were in fourth grade, or where a significant proportion of the kids scored in the satisfactory range when it came to high school math) seemed pathetic if their scores had not gone up. The underlying expectation is that academic performance is always and only a matter of comparison.

Journalists, too, have played a significant role in persuading us to think of education primarily as a means to wealth. Many years ago, I called the *New York Times* to propose a regular series describing how teachers ply their craft and solve everyday teaching problems. The editor in charge of the education section, with whom I spoke, was enthusiastic. She said to me, "You know, we're always so busy covering the big topics in education, we rarely get to report on teaching." There wasn't a hint of irony or surprise in her voice when she said this. From her perspective, what actually went on inside classrooms was more of a human-interest angle, one they could ill afford to focus on. Startled by what she said, I began keeping tabs on the big education-related stories and editorials in major newspapers. Sure enough, most of the articles were about policy (the opening and closing of charter schools, the appointment of school chancellors, the politics of school boards, and of course the debate about testing). But the most common theme was money. Journalists exhort us to fund education because by doing so we'll raise the standard of living, close the income gap, or improve our global standing.

New York Times columnist Thomas L. Friedman is one of the most ardent editorial voices about education. He has argued vociferously that it is more important for children to be curious and passionate than to know a lot about specific topics. However, he frames these values in terms of their economic worth:

> We know that it will be vital to have more of the "right" education than less, that you will need to develop skills that are complementary to technology rather than ones that can be easily replaced by it and that we need everyone to be innovating new products and services to employ the people who are being liberated from routine work by automation and software. The winners won't just be those with more I.Q. It will also be those with more P.Q. (passion quotient) and C.Q. (curiosity quotient) to leverage all the new digital tools to not just find a job, but to invent one or reinvent one, and to not just learn but to relearn for a lifetime.[16]

His ideas for revamping our schools rest for the most part on an economic argument. His point is that if our schools (and students) fall behind, it will hurt our financial security, both at an individual level and as a nation in competition with other nations.[17]

Money has infiltrated our schools through another portal as well. Bankers and businesspeople have decided that they are the ones to improve our schools. In 2010 the educational historian Diane Ravitch did a dramatic about-face regarding educational testing and the promise of charter schools.[18] Having been a loud and influential proponent of both (among other things, she worked in the administration of George H.W. Bush), in recent years she began to see that the national obsession with tests was in fact corrupting rather than improving the process of education in our schools. She also began to think that charter schools were sucking the lifeblood out of the public school system as well as allowing business interests to shape what was happening in classrooms. In her book *The Death and Life of the Great American School*

System, she documents some of the ways that people in business and finance have been wielding their influence and sidelining the input of parents and teachers. The signs of this influence are not always subtle or ephemeral either. They can be seen and heard within the halls and classrooms of schools all over the country.

One of the most insidious examples of this influence is the Edison Project, a for-profit school management company founded by Chris Whittle in the early 1990s. Whittle's plan was to start a whole fleet of new charter schools, as well as take over existing public schools, in order to replace what he saw as flawed educational practices with superior ones. At its inception, Edison wore the mask of innovation. The schools would be lively, effective, and well run. The people in charge, freed from the bureaucracy of school boards, the dulling effects of lifetime educators, and the dreariness of existing school curricula, would reinvent education. Good people were involved in the project, among them Benno Schmidt, former president of Yale University. This group, seemingly well-intentioned, made articulate and compelling statements about the goals of the Edison Project. In describing the program, Schmidt said, "We also looked to the future: the sound use of state-of-the-art technology and how to organize educational spaces that free students' minds rather than constrain them."[19] The scheme embraced the idea that school would liberate children to become discerning, creative, and open-minded. The group's motto clearly expressed the project's biases: "The Edison Project believes that the creative, entrepreneurial forces so vital in other areas of our society can breathe new life into public education." In other words, schools would be better if entrepreneurs and businesspeople took over.

The project shimmered with idealism about children and their future. The only hitch was that each of the classrooms in which these lucky children would be educated had to contain a television offering programming designed by Whittle's company, as well as the advertisements that produced income for the company. The idealism of freeing children's minds was anchored by a purely profit-driven motive: inculcate children with ads. Along with a sense of possibility, the scent of money wafted through the Edison plan. Here is the announcement of the first Edison schools, which opened in 1998, as described in a brief article in the *New York Times*:

> *Edison Project Gets Aid to Open New Schools*
> With the help of a new $25 million grant, the Edison Project, the New York company that seeks to operate public schools for a profit, announced yesterday that it would double the size of its business this fall to forty-eight schools in twenty-five cities nationwide. The unusual philanthropic boon came from a new foundation established by Donald G. and Doris Fisher, owners of The Gap clothing chain of San Francisco. The $25 million, which will be used to subsidize California school districts that want to hire the Edison Project, will create fifteen autonomous public schools, known as charter schools. Four are scheduled to open this fall: two in Ravenswood in Northern California, one in the Napa Valley, and one in West Covina, in Southern California.[20]

As things turned out, the Edison Project largely failed. The company lost control of the vast majority of schools it had taken over. The students who had attended Edison schools did not do better on tests or complete school at a higher rate than children in other schools, as Whittle had so confidently promised. Its only visible current project is an expensive and exclusive private school in Manhattan.

Programs like the Edison Project pushed education further along the money trail. In the past few decades, money has taken on a new role. It is no longer just the intended outcome of an education or the measure of educational success. It has now become the not-so-invisible hand steering the process of education itself, deciding what children should learn and how.

In recent years, the money preoccupation has trickled upward, shaping our ideas about college as well as K–12 schooling. Not so long ago, private college was a luxury that few could afford. But in the nineteenth century, first Horace Mann and then Charles Eliot led the charge to make ability rather than heritage the price of admission to college. Though the intention was to recognize that wealth or lofty ancestry was no guarantee of intellectual ability, motivation, or academic inclination, it also came from the realization that a college degree opened doors and changed one's future trajectory. During the same period, the introduction of excellent state university systems provided another avenue for bright and motivated adolescents with no money to get a college education. But as with K–12 education, when college changed from being a luxury for a few to a necessity for all, it redefined itself. Where once it had been a place to expand one's horizons, read great books, get exposure to new disciplines, and learn how to participate in intellectual discourse, it now became another step toward getting a job or moving up a career ladder. The focus turned from getting a college education to getting a college degree.

Nearly every article that was published in a major newspaper between the years 2010 and 2014 about college education compared its cost to the financial benefit it might offer students in the long run. Most of the economic analyses on the "value" of college focus on a simple question: do people who complete college make more money, have more economic security, and acquire access to better jobs than people who do not complete college? It is easy to understand why the question has been framed this way. It is a lot easier to get job and income data and match those to something as unitary and concrete as a diploma than to figure out how the experiences contained within four years might change the way a person thinks, feels, or approaches the world. And yet, as so often happens, the methods used by researchers end up defining the phenomenon.

But the emphasis on education as a route to money cannot be attributed only to newspapers, researchers, business, and the government. Most individuals think of schooling in terms of money, whether they realize it or not.

I teach a lecture course on education that for many of the approximately fifty students in the class is the first time they have read research about children, and about teaching and learning. We watch videotapes of children in school. We discuss theories of education. We try to come up with curricula, think of better ways to group children, and devise innovative approaches to assessment. Some of the students get so interested in the topic that they sign up for an advanced class I offer, a seminar on teaching and learning. In that class each student spends eight hours a week working in a local classroom. They also participate in weekly seminar discussions and read articles and books about teaching and learning.

One day a young man enrolled in the seminar asked if we could meet to talk after class. When he sat down in my office, he said in a quiet voice, "I love this stuff. I can't stop thinking about it. I know it's what I want to spend my life doing."

"Great!" I said. "Let's talk about some other courses that might take you deeper into the discipline."

"I don't think I can," he answered with an uncertain look on his face. "I love education. I want to teach. But I can't do that to my parents. They worked so hard to get me here. How can I tell them that they did all of that, and I'm just going to be a teacher? I have to go into a lucrative field, something that will ensure a good career. I'm going to study computer programming."

I have heard this sort of thing time and again. And on the face of it, it seems perfectly plausible. If sending a son or daughter to college is a stretch for a family, why shouldn't the student do everything in his or her power to ensure that the college experience is "worth it"? The question is, what do we mean by "worth it"? Would it be less worth it for this family if their son became a teacher who woke up every day eager to go to work and went to bed each night fulfilled by what he had done than if he made lots of money but hated his work?

It is no longer 1848 but 2014. Imagine a small boy moving to this country today, because he and his family have run out of options in their native land. This boy is bright and has lots of energy. His family is kind and hardworking but not distinguished in any way. Perhaps they cannot read. When they arrive in this country they move to a community where others from their homeland have settled before them. But this little boy does not go straight to work, as he might have 150 years ago, the way Andrew Carnegie did. Instead this little boy goes straight to school, like virtually every other child in the United States now does. What will school provide him with, and what paths will it lead him down? What qualities will it nurture and strengthen, and what qualities will be quelled? Do our schools give children an education that will enrich their lives? Of all Carnegie's accomplishments, the one today's schools are most eager to steer children toward is money. And the wild irony is that the odds are overwhelmingly against any of them getting rich. Though attending school dramatically raises a child's chance of earning a decent wage, it's not at all clear that our schools provide any of the experiences that might lead to the other qualities that defined Carnegie: his hunger for information and ideas, his appreciation of books, his commitment to the common good, his sense of perseverance and hard work, his interest in innovation, and his gift for language. We have been learning the wrong lesson from the Andrew Carnegies, Bill Gateses, and Steve Jobses of the world. It's not their wealth that children should aspire to. Nor is the lesson that school is unnecessary for success. Few people will become very rich. But Carnegie achieved other great things that might guide our thinking. He possessed ambition, expertise, ingenuity, thoughtfulness, erudition, and an abiding interest in community. And while it's true he seemed to acquire these qualities in a somewhat quirky and serendipitous way, they needn't be left to chance. They can be acquired through education. And unlike great wealth, they are prizes available to everyone.

A close look inside the classroom door suggests that in the past 150 years we have come to think, perhaps without realizing it, that the purpose of education is to make money. Though going to school hugely increases a child's chance of earning a decent wage in adulthood, that fact need not, and should not, define our thinking about *what* and *how* children should learn. Decent wages may be a very desirable outcome of attending school. But that doesn't mean that money should be the goal of education or the measure of its success. Of course, the skeptic might ask what harm there is in designating money as the purpose of school. As it turns out, plenty.

TWO

How Money
Impoverishes Education

Several years ago I worked with an unusually talented and passionate undergraduate student at Williams College named Rose-Marie. Though she attended Williams, she did not come from privilege. When she was just a little girl, her family had moved from Puerto Rico to a small industrial city in upstate New York. Her father was a policeman, and her mother had worked as a school secretary. Most of the friends and neighbors with whom she had grown up had been poor, and most had emigrated to the United States from Central America. She was smart, vivacious, and brimming with energy and an intense sense of purpose about teaching. She was a natural in the classroom. When I observed her student-teaching in a local third grade, I could see the kind of authority she had with children, a sense of confidence and command that is worth gold in the classroom but which money cannot buy. Her love of teaching radiated from her. If there was ever a college graduate suited by life experience, personality, and education to succeed as a teacher, Rose-Marie was it. But choosing a life in teaching took boldness on her part. Her parents had worked hard to get her to Williams. She was their pride and joy, and they imagined great things for her. They wanted her to be a doctor, not a schoolteacher. But Rose-Marie couldn't give up her passion. She went home for Christmas of her senior year and told them she just had to be a teacher, that it was her calling. Because they loved her, they accepted her decision. Naturally, she got several great offers, and accepted a job at a charter school in New York City. She graduated and went off to scale tall buildings and be a great teacher. In April of her first year, she called me. She needed to talk things through. Her school, located in Harlem, was filled with adorable if underprivileged kids. She'd felt an instant rapport with her students. Many of them had problems, but she could understand what they were struggling with, and she had ideas about how to help them learn—ideas she was sure would work. She liked some of the other teachers too. But she didn't think she was going to make it, she told me.

> This is not a school. It's the military. The children are made to line up all day long. If one foot or hand is out of place, they get a punishment. They aren't allowed to talk at lunch because the teachers say they get out of control. Their reading lessons are so boring. When I suggest an activity that might make reading more fun, my supervisor says there's no time for that, that I must follow the plan already established. This is no place for kids. And it's no place for people who really love teaching.

Rose-Marie told me that she cried about the school at least once a week, that what she was seeing at the school made her wonder what had made her think she would like teaching.

She stuck it out, and at the end of her second year she won a prize for being most promising young teacher in her district. But she soon left that school to teach elsewhere, somewhere less constricted and grim. The story has a happy ending for her, but not for that school, and not for education in general.

Her descriptions recall a passage from *Hard Times* in which Dickens introduces us to Thomas Gradgrind, the headmaster of a school, who explains:

"Now, what I want is, Facts. Teach these boys and girls nothing but Facts. Facts alone are wanted in life. Plant nothing else, and root out everything else. You can only form the minds of reasoning animals upon Facts: nothing else will ever be of any service to them. This is the principle on which I bring up my own children, and this is the principle on which I bring up these children. Stick to Facts, sir!"

The scene was a plain, bare, monotonous vault of a schoolroom, and the speaker's square forefinger emphasized his observations by underscoring every sentence with a line on the schoolmaster's sleeve.

Gradgrind is hell-bent on making sure that his students leave school with the knowledge they need to be "serviceable" in the adult world. Rose-Marie's descriptions were eerily similar. Children were punished for wriggling on line in the halls, chastised for talking to one another, and told again and again to control themselves. When Rose-Marie told her supervisor that she wanted the children to get a kick out of reading, she was informed that love of reading was a luxury these children couldn't afford. Instead they needed to learn the skills that would get them good test scores and ultimately a job.

The Power of SLANT

In 2010 I wrote an op-ed piece that stepped on many people's educational nerves. In it I suggested that the current educational approach in the United States, a strange amalgam of No Child Left Behind and Race to the Top, ran smack in the face of what researchers know about how children develop during the elementary school years. I argued that too many schools were using curricula and teaching methods that were strangling both children and teachers. I used some simple examples:

> In order to design a curriculum that teaches what truly matters, educators should remember a basic precept of modern developmental science: developmental precursors don't always resemble the skill to which they are leading. For example, saying the alphabet does not particularly help children learn to read. But having extended and complex conversations during toddlerhood does. Simply put, what children need to do in elementary school is not to cram for high school or college, but to develop ways of thinking and behaving that will lead to valuable knowledge and skills later on. . . . Children would also spend an hour a day writing things that have actual meaning to them—stories, newspaper articles, captions for cartoons, letters to one another. People write best when they use writing to think and to communicate, rather than to get a good grade.

I went on to argue that we should use a curriculum designed to raise children, not test scores.

The paper and I were flooded with mail. Many of the letters and online responses were ecstatic—teachers, parents, psychologists, and even some high school and college students were relieved and encouraged to encounter an alternative to what they saw as stifling and discouraging methods. But more than a handful of the letters were from people who were outraged by what I was proposing. Most of these came from businesspeople and those involved with charter schools, furious at what they took to be my criticism of their approach: putting great stock in test scores. One letter stood out. It came from a woman who had been in finance all her life and was now part of a philanthropic group supporting a new group of charter schools in Connecticut. She had written me a warm letter just a few months earlier, in response to another piece I had written about teacher training. At that time she'd felt we were kindred spirits. Now, though, she wrote to tell me she felt betrayed. "In our schools, teachers and principals are trying their hardest to raise children's test scores. You make it seem like our classrooms must be dull and rigid. It's not true," she said. "I just can't understand why you would be critical of schools that are trying to help children who have been floundering. Come visit us. You'll see. It's a wonderful place."

I accepted, and took a trip to her one of her schools.

The school was located on a small street in one of the poorer neighborhoods of a small city that is infamous for the conflicts between its rich and poor residents. The minute I walked into the building, I could feel a sense of energy, discipline, and order. I slipped into a science class for fourth graders. A young white teacher, bouncy and enthusiastic, was engaged in a question-and-answer session with her students, all of whom were black. They were for the most part quiet, attentive, and composed. A few of them seemed enthusiastic. The teacher was asking a series of questions about the material they had studied, which was about the structure of cells. If someone raised a hand, she tossed him or her a teddy bear. As long as a student was holding the teddy bear, he or she could answer. When the students finished answering, he or she threw the teddy bear back to the teacher. The children were well behaved, and at least some of them gave the answers the teacher was looking for. I was impressed by their attentiveness, though it seemed to me there was more zeal for throwing and catching the teddy bear than there was for the intricacies of cell division. But still, the mood was focused and pleasant.

Then I wandered into a first-grade classroom where the children were about to begin a new lesson on spelling. The teacher (who was white) was up at the board; the children (who were all black and Latino) were facing her from their desks, which were organized in short rows. She began by pointing to a long banner up on the wall behind her, with big bold letters that read SLANT, which was a mnemonic for "Sit up straight. Lean forward. Act interested. Nod your head. Track the teacher."

Then she went over the instructions for the worksheet in front of them, making sure they knew exactly what to do. Most of the children looked down at the sheet. A few seemed eager to get started; many showed no expression at all.

One little boy wriggled in his chair. "Marco, sit up. Don't wriggle," the teacher said. He looked at her, then down at the sheet. At the very same moment, he shot his right leg out toward the desk next to his. "Marco, sit still. You must focus on your worksheet." Marco looked down at the paper in front of him, and then his gaze drifted to the pencil neatly lying in its groove just above the sheet. He picked it up, rolled it around in his fingers, and then set it down. Next he twisted his head to see what the kids in the row behind him were doing. "Marco, since you cannot sit still, you must stand up now and stand behind your seat." There was a two-second pause while Marco considered this command. So the teacher spoke again. "Marco, did you hear what I said? If you're not able to focus, then you must stand behind your desk, hands on the back of your seat. That's the rule. We must learn how to spell these words." Marco stood up, did a little skip, and then stood behind the desk with his hands in front of him. He knew what to do. They all did. This ritual had clearly occurred many times for many children in this room. Three minutes later, he was told he could now take his seat and resume work.

At this point the teacher was no longer giving instructions to the group; the children were now supposed to be filling in the lines on their worksheet. Marco's butt slid a little way off his chair. "Marco, we must finish these sheets. Sit back down right now and concentrate." She turned away to help another little boy who had come up to ask her a question. Marco didn't sit down. He got up and wandered toward the counter at the back of the room, just near the doorway. He stood for a minute, looking aimless. He peered out the little window in the door, looking toward the hallway, which was empty. His eyes slid across the counter. He noticed the pencil sharpener, which was the old-fashioned metal kind with a crank. He quickly and quietly put one of his fingers inside the pencil hole and began to turn the crank.

Many children have trouble concentrating, following rules, and staying focused on their work. Many teachers struggle to help such children learn how to control themselves and behave well. Books have been written about it. Millions of dollars are spent on research trying to remedy the problem. But the episode I witnessed would not have happened if the goal had been to help this little boy develop some sense of agency or become engaged in interesting work.

Instead, the goal was as clear as the banner on the wall. The children had to fill out the worksheet so that they would learn to spell the words that would appear on their test, so that they could get better test scores, so that they could go to a better high school, so that they could get into college, so that they could get a job. A salary, however far off and seemingly removed from that first-grade classroom, was calling the shots. Asking young children to do things they find boring and difficult so that someday they may earn a decent wage doesn't work. Children aren't able to stifle their natural energies and interests for the sake of a goal that is abstract, distant, and too vague to have any meaning to them in their present and very vivid lives.

When children have good experiences at school, they are encouraged to think and behave in ways that will open doors for them later on. There is no question that schooling plays a vital role in creating social mobility. But training children to be obedient workers is not the way to meet that aspiration.

Now, it's worth acknowledging that there are some children who can and do seem able to keep their eye on the future at all times. These kids take on boring or seemingly meaningless tasks just because they are told to, or because they know it will lead to something good when they are grown up. Often such children come from families who have money and enjoy its advantages. The parents are well educated and have good jobs. The children in such families are saturated with the rewards of deferred pleasures. They spend much of their daily life paving the way for future success by doing well in school, trying to win at a sport, engaging in community service so that their applications to college will be impressive. But even for them, the route shaped by money is often hollow.

Recently, one of my students, a senior at Williams College named Julia, came in to talk to me about her four years as an undergraduate. She grew up in an educated and privileged family. Both her parents went to elite colleges. She came to Williams with vivid ambition and aspirations. She loved college. But she also began to question the path she's been on since she was a little girl, she told me.

As a senior in college, I have spent over 72 percent of my life in school. Education has been an integral, instrumental, and inescapable part of the past sixteen years. It is the focal point around which my development, family, and friends revolve.

As I conclude the penultimate semester of my undergraduate education and attempt to enter the job market, intruding doubts about the purpose of my significant dedication to school creep into my mind. The hesitation feels familiar, but after sixteen years, I know how to deal with these questions. The solution is a simple, linear mantra: *I go to school to get a good education to get a good job to be successful to make enough money to be happy.*

This shallow succession of goals did little to quiet my doubts about the aim of my valued and expensive education and is certainly unsatisfactory now, but it often succeeded in subduing suspicion long enough for me to turn in an assignment or study for an exam—and I am not an exception. The supposed connection between school, money, and happiness has and continues to serve as a justification for my peers, our parents, and our communities. I remember dragging my way through geometry class freshman year of high school. I was bored, frustrated, and indignant. "What is the point?" I thought. "When will I ever have to use this?" The answer, thus far, has seemingly been never, and as a fourteen-year-old, I had a sinking suspicion that would be the case. And yet I trudged forward. I had to take geometry to eventually take calculus so I could get into a good school and get a good education, then I would get a good job and be successful and make enough money to be happy. My goal, at that point, was not an immediate understanding, a focused inquiry, or even a moment of personal success. My goal, the goal of my education, was years down the line, tied up in some vague idea involving a career defined as successful by the value of the paycheck attached.

She's not the only one trapped on the wrong escalator.

Can You Be Happy as a Cab Driver?

A few years ago, I was teaching a seminar called Childhood in Context. Our goal each semester was to try to identify the ways in which children are shaped by their environments (their families, their geography, their nation). Every Tuesday and Friday afternoon, eighteen students and I met to talk about articles, films, and data. My students were a varied bunch, as they always are. Some came from wealthy families and were the third or fourth generation to attend Williams. Many came from middle-class professional families, with parents who were doctors, lawyers, and schoolteachers. Some parents worked in advertising, retail, or manufacturing. One student's father was a mailman, and one a mason. Another student's mother was a member of the clergy. Many came from suburban towns in the United States. But one student came from Zimbabwe, another from Argentina, and one from Cuba. Three were the first in their family to attend college. As a group, the class was lively and engaged, eager to think about how the studies we read did or did not connect to their own experiences. I had just shown them the first installment of Michael Apted's classic film series that began with 1964's *Seven Up*. That year Apted had filmed a group of seven-year-old children in the United Kingdom, and since then he had returned every seven years to film the same individuals again as they grew older. I wanted my students to consider the various paths children's lives take by the time they are young adults.

Each of the films in the series begins with a famous quote: "Show me a child at seven, and I will show you the man." Apted's real interest is in the way in which social class in Great Britain shapes people's life stories—the upper-class children who attend Eton and Cambridge, just as their parents did before them; the working-class kids who never leave their hometowns, the ones who struggle with money, broken homes, mental illness, and disappointment; and the few who break out of the path set by their social class, discovering a new way to live. My students were riveted. They zeroed in on one of the more charismatic stories, about a boy named Tony. In the first sequences of the film Tony jumps off the screen, a feisty little seven-year-old who tussles with other children, has dirt on his cheeks, and speaks with a strong East End accent. By the time he is fourteen years old, Tony says that all he cares about is fulfilling his lifelong dream of becoming a jockey. He proudly tells the filmmaker, and the audience, that he has gotten a job at the racetrack, running the bets back and forth, and that he believes this is the first step in working his way up to a chance as a jockey. We next see Tony as a young man of twenty-one. He is a compact man, and still vividly working class in his accent and his manner, which is both ebullient and belligerent. He explains that though he rode in one horse race, he failed as a jockey, and so he left that life behind him. Instead, he tells us, he is now married, and he's been preparing for The Knowledge, the intensely challenging test London cab drivers must pass in order to get their license. Work as a cab driver offers a middle-class wage, which provides a very decent life. Cab drivers in London typically send their children to university, read, travel, and attend the theater. I tell my students that in subsequent films in the series we see that Tony and his wife go on to have three children, and that Tony buys a pub with a few partners, in order to augment his work as a cab driver.

My students are saddened by his story. One says, "He had to give up his dream." The others nod in agreement. Another says, "Clearly his aspirations were stifled because of his social class."

That trips me up. I detect an important and unspoken assumption simmering just beneath the surface, and so I ask, "What makes being a jockey a higher aspiration than being a cab driver?"

For a split second they look startled. How strange for me to question that assumption, their looks tell me. But then a young man speaks out, saying in a rush, "You could become the best jockey around. But who ever heard of the best cab driver?" In one simple sentence he was telling me something important about how young people in 2014 regard their futures. If they were smart enough or lucky enough to get into Williams, they'd better aim high. They'd better make *use* of their education. But what did it mean to him, and the others in the class, to aim high, to make use of college? I probed further. For them, it was clear: aiming high meant to get the highest-paying job they could, to do things that would make them famous, powerful, and rich. The students in that class, every single one of them, accepted the idea that the "better" your education, the "higher" you should aim professionally. And they pretty much agreed on what "better" and "higher" meant. They may not have come from the same families, neighborhoods, or economic brackets, but they all had the same view of where their schooling should take them. When I pushed back, asking them, "What if Tony is happy as a cabdriver? What if his life is actually better doing something that doesn't break his heart like being a jockey? What if the higher aspiration is not the thing that makes you rich or famous, the one you can beat others at, but the thing that gives you contentment?," they tilted their heads at me and squinted slightly, as if trying to get me back in focus. What the hell was I talking about? However, just under the surface, many students are already struggling with the vise created by the formula my senior described.

Take, for example, a student I'll call Javier. He is tall and good-looking, with the easy grace of a young athlete, and when I first met him, in one of my courses, he seemed quite interested in children and in psychological development. He made it clear by the second class meeting that his experiences as an immigrant from a Central American country gave him unusual insights into the topics we were considering. By the fourth class I realized he wasn't doing any of the readings, and that when he spoke, which was often, he never ever mentioned any of the readings. Instead, he based his comments on personal experiences. The more our discussions focused on the scientific issues that lay at the core of the topic, the more I could feel his interest fading. By the fourth week he was skipping class regularly. Then I read his first paper. It was terrible—obviously something he had dashed off in an evening, without even a rewrite. What really pulled me up short, however, was that he missed class the day I handed the papers back. Nor did he ask about it until several weeks later, when I gave out the assignment for the second paper. Clearly he only wanted to know the grade he had gotten to see how close to the edge he was. He seemed to disappear a little more with every class meeting. And then in December, during the last week of class, he realized he might not pass. He asked to come talk to me.

I was blunt with him: "You seem to be phoning it in, Javier."

He nodded, and his gaze veered off, settling on the light switch on the wall behind my desk. "Ever since I was a little boy," he said, "all I've cared about was baseball and football. I've never been interested in anything else. None of this here interests me at all."

I asked in a gentler voice than I had used before, "But may I ask, if those are the things you care most about, and you care nothing for academics, what are you doing *here*?"

His eyes filled with tears, and he shrugged as if both regretful and slightly mystified. "My mother thought it was a good opportunity," he told me. And, of course, in one sense it is. Getting a degree from an elite college will help Javier get a good job. On the other hand, his father is an attorney, so it's not as if this particular college represented his only possible means of entry into a middle-class life. But he has just spent four years doing things he doesn't care about, and missing the opportunity to get good at something he does care about. Now, as he nears graduation, he hasn't even figured out what it is he would like to be good at. The lure of a lucrative job has drawn him away from the benefits of an education that would prepare him for a satisfying job, one he might really care about. But this financial funnel doesn't start in college, or even in the senior year of high school. It begins long before, in kindergarten.

Real Reading Versus Fake Reading

In 1955 Rudolph Flesch, an Austrian-born man with a PhD in English from Columbia University, wrote a book that rattled every parent's cage and stirred up huge debate within U.S. schools: *Why Johnny Can't Read, and What You Can Do About It*.[1] Flesch argued that we were teaching children to read the wrong way. At the time, most schools in this country used a method called "look, say." The "look, say" method was simple: show children the same word over and over, asking them to repeat it again and again, until they had in effect memorized it. Children were encouraged to notice the shape of the word, to use clues about a word based on the rest of the sentence (the meaning), and to use visual hints from any accompanying illustration. Soon their ability to recognize those words would enable them to recognize new unfamiliar words. This is sometimes referred to as the sight method, since it's based on a child's recognition of various visual clues plus a growing mental store of well-known words. Flesch argued that without learning the sounds of letters and letter combinations, children would be stymied, dependent on deciphering various kinds of visual information and on their own memory for familiar words. Instead, he argued that children should learn how to sound words out phonetically. His premise was that helping children understand the underlying mechanics of our phonetic system would make them much stronger readers, armed with the tools for learning any new word they came across. Thinking, rather than memory, would form the basis of their reading process.

The conflict between these two approaches was historic, with teachers and school systems battling over the merits of each approach. Each side was so vehement that the dispute became known as the "reading wars." That was sixty years ago. But this debate is no mere relic from the past. In recent decades those who argue that children should learn to read by recognizing words in context rebranded their approach as "whole language," a label with more child-friendly connotations. Whole-language advocates have argued that children are so slowed down by the process of sounding words out (the phonetic approach) that by the time they get to the end of the sentence they've forgotten what it is about or have simply lost interest. Phonics proponents argue that the whole-language approach leaves many children mystified, unable to crack the code on their own. The war still rages on. The passage below is from an article published in 2007, describing reading battles in Wisconsin:

> Surrounded by five first graders learning to read at Hawthorne Elementary here, Stacey Hodiewicz listened as one boy struggled over a word. "Pumpkin," ventured the boy, Parker Kuehni. "Look at the word," the teacher suggested. Using a method known as whole language, she prompted him to consider the word's size. "Is it long enough to be pumpkin?" Parker looked again. "Pea," he said, correctly.
>
> Call it the $2 million reading lesson. By sticking to its teaching approach, that is the amount Madison passed up under Reading First, the Bush administration's ambitious effort to turn the nation's poor children into skilled readers by the third grade. The program, which gives $1 billion a year in grants to states, was supposed to end the so-called reading

wars—the battle over the best method of teaching reading—
but has instead opened a new and bitter front in the fight.

According to interviews with school officials and a string
of federal audits and e-mail messages made public in recent
months, federal officials and contractors used the program to
pressure schools to adopt approaches that emphasize phonics,
focusing on the mechanics of sounding out syllables, and to
discard methods drawn from whole language that play down
these mechanics and use cues like pictures or context to teach.
Federal officials who ran Reading First maintain that only
curriculums including regular, systematic phonics lessons had
the backing of "scientifically based reading research" required
by the program.[2]

Studies and experiments examining how children learn to
read have piled up as high as the Grand Tetons. Millions of dollars have been earned and squandered by textbook companies
and departments of education. Entire careers have been made
and lost on the grounds of this war. And yet we're still on the
wrong track.

Not long ago, I spent some time observing a group of four
elementary school classrooms in Massachusetts. The first-grade
classrooms were sunny and cheerful. Each classroom had small
tables and chairs, enough for every student. Each classroom had
a reading corner, shelves for paper, crayons, scissors, pencils, various kinds of math equipment, and interesting games (Lotto, puzzles, and Scrabble). Two of the classrooms had aquariums, and
all of them had pictures on the wall. Any young parent looking
around for a town with a nice school for their children would like
what they saw. The teachers in these classrooms were friendly—
they liked children, used friendly voices when talking to their
students, and gave help when help was needed. You could see that
they were making a real effort to make various academic routines

more fun—spelling, addition, reading words out loud, writing sentences, and following instructions.

Over several weeks I watched carefully to see what children were doing to become better readers. Every day the children practiced spelling words, usually focusing on some particular challenge: long vowels, words that begin with three consonants (such as *str*), and tricky vowel combinations (fr*ie*nd, b*ui*ld, etc.). They practiced reading messages aloud—the calendar, a note from the teacher, the weather report. They read short, simple stories in order to answer brief questions about whatever they had just read. At first, it all looked pretty good to me—happy, busy classrooms where children were working on the building blocks of academic success. But by the second week, it dawned on me that something important was missing. With all the attractive materials, jolly circle times, and sensible work, there was one thing the children were barely doing at all: I almost never encountered children choosing books they were eager to plunge into and sitting down in a comfortable place where they could read for a long time.

Finally, in early November, after two and a half months of no real reading, I broached the subject with the teachers. "I'm curious," I began. "There's so much good stuff going on in this class. But I haven't noticed children getting many opportunities to read, and I haven't seen you read aloud to them very often." One of the first-grade teachers paused for moment, as if to mentally review the past ten weeks, then said, "Yeah, I guess they don't get much time for that. I used to give them much more time to read, and I used to read aloud to them every afternoon. But there's just not enough time in the day. Too much else going on. For one thing, the DIBELS [Dynamic Indicators of Basic Early Literacy Skills] takes up a lot of our time. Between assessing them and practicing to improve, it really leaves no time for books."

DIBELS is a program developed by researchers at the Center for Teaching and Learning at the University of Oregon. A key finding of the group was that the speed and fluency with which children can read words aloud when they are young (say, between the ages of five and seven) predicts how well they will read when they are older. The original program was designed to identify children at risk for reading problems so that teachers could intervene before a child began to fall behind, compounding the original difficulty. The test is a fairly reliable predictor of later reading skills, at least as those skills are measured by standardized reading tests. This should come as no surprise to anyone.

The six-year-old child who can fluently and easily read off a list of words is more likely to read competently when she is twelve than the little boy who at age six reads the words out slowly or stumbles over certain letter combinations. Whatever causes a given child to struggle at the beginning stage of the reading process (problems matching sounds with letters, problems seeing the letters correctly, or difficulty building up a big repertoire of familiar words) is likely to still be a part of a child's mental makeup as she develops. Moreover, the child who struggles in first grade is going to get far less daily practice reading real pages and stories. By the time she is in fourth grade she's simply had less experience reading than another child. Similarly, a child whose reading difficulties are caused by something more pervasive and general, such as growing up in a family where no one else can read, is also likely to struggle more than children who grow up in literate households. In other words, there is no magic to the fact that problems identifying words at age five or six predict later problems reading.

The original idea behind the DIBELS test was similar to the idea behind the first IQ test, which was developed in France by Alfred Binet. Binet created the IQ test in order to identify schoolchildren who were likely to struggle academically, so that teachers could give them the help they needed to learn. Like the IQ test, DIBELS is also intended to identify children who are likely to struggle, in this case specifically with reading, so that they can get extra help before third grade and therefore become able readers.

But that's not how DIBELS has come to be used in many schools. Instead of serving as a diagnostic tool, to help teachers address the specific language and reading needs of each student, DIBELS tests are now used as an end in themselves. Teachers labor under the impression that if their students' DIBELS scores improve, all will be well. But improving a child's test score is not at all the same as helping the child with the underlying problem that lead to the original low score. When the first-grade teacher explained that DIBELS had pushed authentic reading out of her classroom, she spoke as if what she was saying made total sense. From her perspective, reading books aloud and giving children time to read to themselves was a luxury they couldn't afford as long as they continued to do poorly on the DIBELS test. Instead, it seemed more targeted and efficient to her to use that time to practice DIBELS items. But while identifying and calling out as many words as he can in one minute might help a six-year-old get a better score on the DIBELS test next time he takes it, such practice will not make him a better or more avid reader.

Teachers commonly end up spending so much time administering and scoring DIBELS tests and so much time drilling their children on the DIBELS words that they end up reducing the amount of time children spend reading. This is a travesty, given what the research has actually taught us about what it takes for a child to become a reader. Abundant evidence elucidates what I heard a ninety-year-old reading teacher from San Francisco say many years ago: "Every child learns to read just a little differently." Her point was that systems don't teach children to read. Books and sustained time reading with expert readers is what helps children learn to read. This is the secret behind the reading wars. When the whole language approach works—when a child seems to easily recognize words in context—it's because he or she internalizes the mechanics of reading (including the phonetic system) without realizing it, using what psychologists call implicit learning. That hidden and seemingly fluid process is most likely to occur under certain conditions: when a child has parents who read, when she can instantly "hear" the sound of each letter, and when she finds it easy to recognize written symbols. In other words, a child with no specific neurological barriers (reading disabilities) and a literate background is likely to pick up the phonetic system couched within the whole-language approach. Similarly, when children are not slowed down by the somewhat laborious and tedious process of learning phonics, it is because the process comes easily and quickly to them, allowing them to skip right on to a version of sight reading before the whole thing becomes distasteful. The psycholinguist Frank Smith has insisted that the best way to learn to read is simply by reading. Most children, given exposure to books and reading and offered plenty of opportunity to read, spontaneously use the processes buried in both the whole-language and phonics approaches. So what most children need, whether they draw upon sight words or phonics, is the chance to practice reading—a lot.[3]

With DIBELS, what began as a useful diagnostic tool has become an obstacle to real literacy. Years ago, I observed a little boy who seemed to have intractable reading problems. Then his teacher invited him to read aloud to her dog, who came to school with her each day. That did the trick. He liked reading to the dog so much he gladly did it every day. By the end of third grade, he was a competent reader. He was lucky. He had a resourceful and flexible teacher who wanted him to become a reader more than she wanted him to do well on a test.

All of that time spent practicing DIBELS will not make a child into a better reader. And even when such a drill does help a child with the mechanics of reading, it is unlikely to turn a nonreader into a reader. The goal, after all, should ensure not only that children *can* read but also that they *do* read. It's very unlikely that several years of DIBELS or its kin will turn children into avid readers. And here's a paradox: because children who come from families of nonreaders are at higher risk for illiteracy, the temptation is to give those children more drill and less free reading time than might be given to other, more privileged children. But actually, the less literate a child's family, the more important it is to help that child love reading and see it as a valuable resource and satisfying pastime.

Recently I met a young man I'll call Dwight. He was the first in his family to go to college, and he had decided to become a schoolteacher, earning his certification in high school math. By the time I met him, he was teaching ninth- and tenth-grade math in a suburban high school. But when it came time for him to take the tests that would make him eligible for senior status as a teacher, he stumbled. The math components were no problem, but he kept failing the English component of the test. The things he found difficult are unsettling. For instance, when asked to indicate which were complete sentences and which were not, he had trouble. He didn't see why "Until the toys are picked up from the floor" was not actually a sentence. If you read a lot, you don't need to study the rules of sentence identification in order to know when you encounter a line of words that are not a complete sentence. But Dwight had not read much at all. Though he had done all the practicing and drills required in his schools and had passed all his classes successfully, he hadn't read enough to have a feel for what constitutes a real sentence.

Slowly, without realizing it, teachers, principals, and superintendents have been nudged into thinking that getting a certain score on a reading test merits more classroom time than fostering the very abilities the tests are supposed to tap into. A fixation on long-term results, with success looming in an indefinite future, causes teachers (and parents) to sacrifice the present, to ignore the students themselves and what they should be doing *in the present*. The pot of gold may not be visible, but it has a profound impact in the daily lives of students. Each time teachers put a happy-face sticker on a child's worksheet or test, they might just as well use a sticker with a dollar sign on it.

How Will I Use This Later?

When I was seven, I had a teacher named Mr. Harry. He urged us to call him that because he thought it was friendlier and more informal than calling him by his last name (Mr. Hodgkins) and yet more respectful than just calling him Harry. He had wavy dark hair and thick-rimmed glasses. He looked a little like Delmore Schwartz, without any of the brilliance or charisma. The school was progressive, inspired by ideas from John Holt and Herb Kohl, so the teachers were encouraged to teach different things to different children. We were often asked to work independently. One day Mr. Harry decided that my best friend, Gwen, and I should learn long division. He kneeled down between our seats at the table and worked through a problem, explaining each step. I nodded at each demonstration, confident that I was following along. Then he handed us worksheets with twelve long-division problems and left us to it. My friend set to it almost instantly, working her way through the problems. I, however, just sat there dumbly, looking at the page, without understanding anything. I was completely mystified about how to proceed. What had seemed clear to me when Mr. Harry was talking was shrouded in fog the minute I was on my own. After thirty minutes or so, Mr. Harry returned to us, saying with a bright sunny smile, "How are you two doing?" He glanced over Gwen's work with a pleased expression on his face. Then he saw my sheet, completely blank. His face darkened, his mouth curved down, and he said with fury, "What have you been doing all this time? What's wrong with you? You have to learn long division!" I had never struggled with a school task before. But I had no idea how to do long division. I felt miserable at my own incomprehension, terrified by his anger, and humiliated. I asked if I could go to the bathroom, where I promptly locked myself in and cried until I threw up into the toilet. For years I have told that story to my college students as a way of getting us to think collectively about how teaching and learning can go wrong, and why. But the story raises a more basic question, and it's one that plagues our educational system: Why do we teach math? What goal did Mr. Harry have in mind for me?

Frank Morgan is a mathematician who studies bubbles. Among his colleagues in mathematics, his topic is more accurately considered to be geometry. Frank is a very slender man, with fine hair that is so pale it seems white. For many years I couldn't decide if he was in his early thirties or his late fifties. Asking led nowhere. At some point I was told by others that he doesn't believe in age and won't tell you his own, no matter how well intentioned or casual your inquiry. He is credited with transforming the department of mathematics at the elite liberal arts college where he has taught for many years. He accomplished this by training his laser-like focus on the importance of dynamic, engaged, and devoted teachers who would bring mathematics alive for the students.

He is eccentric, no doubt about it. When I first encountered him he wore a bow tie to campus each day. He begins almost every scholarly presentation or public lecture by dipping one of those little colored plastic bubble sticks into a small five-and-dime bottle of bubble soap and blowing bubbles toward his audience, no matter if they are scholars, college students, elementary school students, or just ordinary town residents attending a community lecture. Much of what he says in his lectures (including in his classes) is announced with the ceremony and formality of someone who is about to perform an amazing magic trick. I have watched him teach and often heard him speak about math education. Two things I heard him say are emblazoned into my memory.

The first came during a seminar I had organized in which scholars from seven different fields (literature, German, biology, astronomy, chemistry, psychology, and mathematics) gathered to talk about how people in their disciplines go from novice to expert. In that setting, Frank pronounced one day with his ceremonial flair, "God created people so that they could appreciate the beauty of mathematics." I was not surprised to hear him refer to God. I knew he had a strong spiritual life. My first reaction was simply to be amazed that anyone could think mathematics was so beautiful it required a species just to fully appreciate it.

My second thought was how lucky a math student would be to have a teacher who felt that way about his subject matter, especially a topic that to many of us is about as appealing as a trip to the dentist.

Ideas about why and how we teach math in this country could give you whiplash. Sometimes the prevailing view is that the majority of children should learn to use math for practical purposes—to balance a checkbook, to read a graph, and to understand their taxes. But of course, this doesn't explain why we require most children to take algebra and geometry in high school. Sit in any high school counselor's office and listen to the reasons given. A sulky fourteen-year-old, hair hanging down over her face as she slouches in the counselor's office, says plaintively, "*Whyyy* do I have to take algebra? I *haate* math. What's the point of it?" The counselor says with authority, "You need two years of math to get into college. And besides, algebra will help you a lot on the SATs." Teachers and counselors across the country are certain that spending two years on something you hate is fine if it might lead to a good score on a test that itself is only a conduit to something else. For students who have grown up assuming they will go to college, this explanation often works. Like Julia, the student quoted at the beginning of this chapter, they accept the idea that a lot of what they do in high school is simply paving the way for what they will do next. But that justification doesn't make them like math; more important, it doesn't help them actually learn math.

The day I threw up over long division, I began hating math, and also stopped learning it. Then when I was fourteen I went to a public high school, where I enrolled in the algebra class. I was told Mrs. McMahon was the toughest, strictest teacher in the school and that it was going to be especially hard for me because of the "hippie math" I had had before. Mrs. McMahon was firm, organized, and emphatic. She was also clear as a bell. Algebra turned out to be a snap for me—I got a 100 on the New York State Regents Examination. My family and teachers were stunned. But I was not surprised. I hadn't needed to understand a thing; all I'd had to do was follow my teacher's crystal-clear instructions. If I could do the procedures, I could ace the test. Math was easy . . . as long as I didn't want to actually understand anything.

The two reasons that children (and their parents) are given for learning math (that it's practical or that it will get you into college) are both bad ones. Neither inspires an interest in learning, and neither encourages a student to think like a mathematician. Framing math lessons in terms of either practicality or college admissions fails to lead children to learn real mathematics. Perhaps that is why so few people in the United States actually use algebraic, geometric, or statistical thinking in any authentic way in their everyday lives.

If the only reason people had to learn math was to balance their checkbooks, they could learn it by the time they were twelve, with a lot less fuss. And to ask students to spend years and years learning procedures and formulae for some distant goal (like a calculus course they might take in college) that may or may not have meaning to them is pointless. Most children cannot focus on such long-term abstract goals. Conjure up a typical thirteen-year-old, blemishes and all, consumed by various kinds of longing, dulled by the presence of rules and adults, transported by the energy of the group, desperate to feel totally engaged. Thirteen-year-olds who cannot envision themselves in college are certainly not going to get it. Thirteen-year-olds who do see college in their future will do it only in terms of one utilitarian goal—they learn math not to understand it but in order to do well on a test.

Many years ago, in a classic study, the psychologists Mark Lepper and David Green invited schoolchildren to draw with crayons. Some of the children were told that they would receive a small prize for their drawing.[4] Other children were not told this but did in fact receive a prize when they finished. A third group of children was told nothing at all. A few days later each of these children was given another opportunity to draw. Lo and behold, the children who had not been rewarded for their drawings were more eager to draw again and spent more time doing it. Equally important, trained raters judged their drawings as more complex and interesting. But one other detail of the study stands out. The children who were promised a prize ahead of time did the least interesting drawings and were the least eager to continue drawing. The moral is pretty clear: an activity that might on its own be rewarding is rendered unappealing when a prize is offered. Why would this be so?

The answer can be found in an altogether different line of work. As far back as the 1960s Elliot Aronson and his colleagues carried out a series of experiments to understand how the concept of cognitive dissonance helps explain people's behaviors and their interpretation of events.[5] In one classic version of this research, college students were asked to spend a few hours doing a boring and menial task such as sorting buttons or screwing caps on small bottles. Some subjects were paid for their efforts, and others were not. After they had finished their "work" each subject was asked to say what he or she thought of the task and how he or she had felt while doing it. Many people, hearing some version of this scenario, are quick to guess that subjects who were paid would like the work more. It makes sense, right? Why wouldn't you prefer an activity that brought you money? If a task is inherently boring, doesn't it sweeten the task to offer some reward? And yet the opposite is true. Not only did the subjects who were not paid rate it more highly than the others did, but they found all kinds of interesting ways to characterize the task as pleasant or worthwhile ("It's soothing," "I feel I'm getting something done," "It gives me time to think," and so on). Why would this be so?

Dissonance theory predicts that people are uncomfortable when one of their actions contradicts some central aspect of their self-concept. Furthermore, people like to think of themselves as good and as consistent. When faced with the dissonance caused by a conflict between a behavior or thought and that self-concept of goodness and consistency, they are motivated to reduce the dissonance by adding some explanation or by reframing their behavior so that it no longer threatens their sense of self. If you do a menial or dull task and are paid for it, you can explain it away in terms of the money ("Of course a smart person like me would be willing to do this silly job for money"). But to do it without a reward might suggest a less pleasing thought ("Why would a smart person like me do dull work for no reason?"). Thus most people quickly and unconsciously justify it ("It's actually quite relaxing," "It's satisfying to get the job done," "I like the time to daydream"). Research has shown that the inverse is true as well. When children are offered concrete rewards for an activity that is already meaningful or pleasurable, they begin to question its intrinsic value. When we entice young children to draw, solve problems, or read by offering them some reward (whether it's a candy, a smiley-face sticker, or the promise of success later on), they have little reason to attend to what they like about doing it. Soon enough they begin to think it's worth doing only when it comes with a prize.

When children are taught that math is worthwhile only because of the dollars it will bring them later on, they are also taught that there is no real satisfaction to be had in understanding the world through numbers or logical relationships. They are encouraged to think of math as a mere tool, a means to an end, rather than as a way of thinking that brings its own pleasures and rewards.

The second unforgettable thing Frank Morgan said was, "My first choice as a college professor would be to work with students who were well taught in mathematics before they got here. My second choice would be students who hadn't had any formal math education at all. My third choice would be students who have been taught the wrong kind of mathematics, and that is what I mostly get." When we frame mathematics in terms of practical tasks, such as balancing a checkbook, we squander an opportunity and, worse, misrepresent mathematics education. When we frame K–12 mathematics as a necessary step to future success, we convince students it has no inherent value. What do we end up with? Children who hate math, and adults who do not have the thinking skills a real mathematical education would have provided.

The Hidden Costs of Money

In June 2007 the *New York Times* published an article with the eye-catching title "Schools Plan to Pay Cash for Marks."[6] For some the headline put into words what seemed to be common sense: if you want students to get good marks, pay them. What better incentive? For others, the headline represented their worst fears: that schools had simply become another embodiment of marketplace mentality.

The article described the work of a promising young economist named Roland Fryer, who was granted tenure at Harvard before he turned thirty. His interest in the role of incentives landed him a job with Joel Klein, then the chancellor of schools for the city of New York. He was hired to help figure out how to get minority children more invested in their schoolwork. Under the plan Fryer devised for New York City, ten-year-old students would get $5 for taking each of ten standardized tests offered throughout the year, and $25 for each perfect score they received. For thirteen-year-olds, the prize was even higher: $10 for each test taken, $50 for each perfect score.

In its first year, the program involved nine thousand schoolchildren. The program at that point cost the city $1.5 million. Was it worth it? The program was assessed twice, first in 2007–8 and again a year later, and the results were, to say the least, underwhelming.

To his credit, Fryer was the first to admit that the program did not lead to higher test scores or better attendance, his two measures of success. Though test scores didn't go up, it was conceivable that the children, lured at first by money, might become more interested in learning, or find that they liked trying hard and wanted to continue trying. However, the data suggested otherwise. Researchers found that the children continued to be clueless about how to get better scores. When interviewed, they mentioned things like test-taking strategies and quick tips for passing the test. Very few of them talked about the content of the material they had encountered. Virtually none of them seemed to understand that learning new ideas or information was the way to get better test scores. Giving children money to learn actually subverted their learning.

A focus on the bottom line undermines education in other un-expected ways as well. In 2010 a fifteen-year-old girl in South Hadley, Massachusetts, named Phoebe Prince hung herself in a stairwell in her home. It became clear that classmates had relent-lessly taunted and threatened her at school. Six teenagers were soon indicted on charges that included statutory rape (for two of the male teenagers involved), violation of civil rights, criminal harassment, disturbance of a school assembly, and stalking. It was also apparent that teachers and administrators had known about at least some of the bullying for a while and had not interceded, or at least had not done so in a way that made any difference. In reaction, states quickly enacted anti-bullying laws. Massachu-setts was among the first to require its schools to come up with policies and procedures that could avert another situation like that of Phoebe Prince. School districts across the nation found themselves scrambling to come up with more effective ways to prevent their students from persecuting one another.

The following year, I was asked to serve on the committee of my local school district as it worked to make its own plan in com-pliance with the new legislation. About twelve of us met every other week for several months. We listed all the ways in which the district already encouraged kindness and punished hurt-fulness. We talked about establishing firmer consequences for children who were mean to others. We debated the difference between a child whose own disturbances made him or her act out with peers and a child who was just a bully. We talked about ways to make peer relationships a more important part of the day. And that's where we hit a wall. Teacher after teacher said, brow wrinkled with worry, "At the beginning of the year, we do some friendship games. And we talk about the importance of kindness in morning meeting. But really, there's not much time in the day to do more than that. Many of the activities recommended by psychologists just aren't realistic. We have too much going on; we cannot fit in one more program or activity."

The bottom line was the bottom line. Under extreme pressure to improve their students' math and English scores, they felt they couldn't really afford the time and effort it would take to devote more resources to helping children get along. A quick scan of schools across the country shows teachers and principals facing the same dilemma. Smaller, incidental efforts to limit bullying and promote cooperation and kindness don't make a real difference. A researcher in Norway named Dan Olweus has shown that in order to change children's behavior toward one another, shift the peer culture, and reduce bullying, a broad, school-wide effort is necessary. But such efforts take time, and time is not limitless. Something else has got to go. And so far, few schools have been willing to sacrifice time on academic skills for social relationships.

However, it's not just that schools find it hard to make room for relationships because of their academic activities. It's often the case that the academic activities themselves undermine young people's impulse to help one another. A high school senior I met recently explained how it works. His school, just south of Los Angeles, has approximately twenty-five hundred students in it. Here is what he says:

> There was a very visible split—the academically minded kids took the APs and were at the top of the class. Everyone else took the basic classes that, in my opinion, didn't do anything at all but babysit them. Within the top half, everyone fought to get into the top ten, and from there, the top five of us fought even harder for the top three spots.
>
> The students in the top ten were usually good friends year to year, but that didn't stop the competition. We never really

studied together (only for the AP exams), we memorized each other's ID numbers so we could look up everyone's grades (they were posted on a wall in each classroom by ID number), would hound our teachers to give us bonus points and to reconsider their grades to us, and would do whatever else possible to get to the top (some students cheated, but I don't think it was that common, at least not for the top five).

The goal was clear: we were going to fight to make it to the top to get into great colleges (the top five of us went to Harvard, UCLA, Williams, Berkeley). It worked for us and has worked every year. The culture was dangerous because of how competitive we were, but it wasn't cutthroat.

This last detail is important. It would be easy to think that only the most vicious and visible forms of competition are a problem. If that were the case, we would be able to identify schools where competition was hindering students' ability to collaborate and help one another. But the truth is, often the competition is subtle and goes hand in hand with a veneer of friendliness that lulls us into thinking it's not really a problem.

Our reluctance to put relationships above individual skill attainment is apparent even in the early grades. In many schools, younger children are discouraged from working together. Teachers understandably assume that when friends work together they'll get silly and lose focus. However, studies have shown that children actually get more done, and learn more, when they are working with a child they like. Teachers also worry that when children work together, the more able student will do the work while the less able child won't learn what she needs to. However, the research suggests a different picture. Studies have shown that less able children often learn a great deal from working with a more knowledgeable or skilled peer. Not only do they achieve more in the short run, but their long-term intellectual development is enhanced. Finally, teachers and parents worry that more able children may be dragged down by working with children who are not as bright. However, again, research shows the opposite. In an elegant series of experiments in both the classroom and the laboratory, Ann Brown from UCLA showed that when children teach one another complex material and ideas, they all learn at a deeper level.[7] In other words, though teachers separate children in the belief that that is the surest route to individual learning, they lose an essential opportunity to foster friendship, collaboration, and altruism. The idea that one must choose skills or social relationships is mistaken. Most educators are working with an implicit set of false assumptions about the value of individual striving and achievement at the expense of an education in collaboration, altruism, and friendship.

Which Executive Is in Control?

When that little boy in Connecticut stuck his finger in the pencil sharpener, he was showing all the signs of what researchers now call low executive function or control. He had trouble focusing (tracking the teacher, listening to the instructions, filling out the worksheet), trouble resisting temptation (swinging his leg toward the child next to him, fiddling with the pencil), and trouble inhibiting his impulses (when he got the impulse to put his finger in the pencil sharpener, he couldn't stop himself). Researchers claim that these three aspects of executive function—focus, the ability to resist temptation, and the ability to inhibit impulses—go hand in hand, in a valuable bundle; children who have good executive function have a big advantage when it comes to success in school, and children who have very little executive control are at serious risk of school failure. Interesting studies are under way to discover if children can learn executive control in school and whether, when it is learned this way, it can change a child's academic prospects. But this focus, while potentially helpful to many children, comes at a price.

Several years ago I was working with the faculty of a suburban school district in Massachusetts. The children there are mostly white, but there is a growing population of families from Central America as well. Though there isn't much racial diversity, there is a lot of economic diversity. The surrounding community is made up mostly of tradespeople and factory workers, but there is also a sizable population of doctors, nurses, lawyers, businesspeople, and teachers. In other words, the district is similar to middle-class communities across the country, and so are the problems its residents face. I had joined the faculty in order to help them find some new ways to improve their teaching practices. I wanted to teach them how to observe children, and how to use such observations as a regular tool for understanding their students. I showed them several different ways to record observations and suggested a wide range of things they might want to observe: how children talk to one another, differences between boys and girls, children's engagement throughout the school day. I spent one whole afternoon helping them learn how to make an objective and detailed record of a child or a group of children. Following this training session, the faculty had six weeks to collect some data. Then we came back together to discuss what they had seen and heard. Nearly two-thirds of the faculty had chosen to make their observations about children's engagement. I wasn't sure whether the choice reflected their interest or their concern. I had suggested several things they should take note of: how often the children they watched became absorbed in something, how long a child or group of children seemed absorbed, and what kinds of things captivated them. When I set this activity up, I had hoped to help them discover whether the students in their school were deeply absorbed frequently or rarely, whether these stretches of engagement lasted a long time or were fleeting, and what kinds of activities elicited such involvement and focus (when the teacher was talking or when the students were working in small groups, more often during hands-on activities or when students were having discussions, and so forth).

When we gathered to compare notes, the teachers seemed excited by what they had done, eager to share their findings with one another. Some reported having seen a lot of engagement in classrooms, while others reported seeing almost none. We put their numbers onto a big graph so we could all look at it together. I was excited and intrigued that their observations had yielded such diversity. So I asked them to talk a little about what they had actually seen, to describe to the group what the students had been doing and how they had expressed their involvement and interest—in other words, to tell one another what the stretches of engagement had looked like. As they took turns sharing their data, one thing became startlingly clear: they hadn't recorded engagement at all. They had been looking for signs of compliance. It turned out that these teachers—young and old, seasoned and novice, men and women, some kind and some bitter—thought that when a child did what she was asked to do or followed a set of instructions, that was a sign of engagement. Again and again, I asked some version of the following: "What about a child who got so lost in an activity he didn't hear what the teacher said?" or "Did you see any children so interested in what was going on in the classroom they didn't get up when the bell rang?" or "What about a child who was so curious about the material that she raised her hand a lot of times to ask more questions about the topic?" or "Did you see any student try to do the same activity several different ways, even if she already had the 'right' answer?"

Again and again, these well-intentioned and skillful teachers made it clear that compliance was the gold standard for their students. Their emphasis is reasonable, given the national focus on the problems caused by noncompliance. Children who can do what they are asked to do tend to stay in school longer, get more out of it, and do better later on in their education than children who consistently fail to follow rules or listen to authority.

But there is more to the story than that. The fervent emphasis on the value of compliance is driven, at least in part, by an educational system that prescribes such specific and concrete goals for all children. If all children must know certain facts about history or be able to solve certain kinds of math problems, it makes sense that getting them all to behave well so that they can learn such material will be at a premium. When learning prescribed material is essential, compliance is efficient. Oddly, this kind of compliance can interfere with a child's ability to concentrate on things out of personal choice. And here we have a paradox: while compliance may lead to good workers, it may not lead to adults who know how to choose something they are interested in and pursue it in the face of obstacles.

Research has made it abundantly clear that engagement is critical to most kinds of success. When children are interested in what they are doing and when they have some sense of what researchers called agency, or self-efficacy, they learn more, and in general they get more out of school. When adults feel engaged with what they do (whether it's their vocation or their avocation) and feel the sense of agency that often goes hand in hand with such absorption, they are much happier. A premium on conformity and obedience has left little room for teaching children something much more powerful: the ability to find activities that are compelling, or to find what is compelling in a task, and thus find a way to become deeply absorbed.

The Two Missing Rs

Not long ago a mother called me, beside herself with frustration. It seems that her fourth-grade son was midway through several days of standardized tests mandated by the state. She had carefully read the notes the school had sent home, urging parents to make sure their children had plenty of sleep and a good breakfast on the days of the tests. Already her hackles were up. Why were sleep and breakfast more important on the days her son would be tested than on the days when he was supposed to be learning things? The answer, I think, is obvious. The school is more worried about how it is doing than how the children are doing. But then she offered the real capper: when the little boy got home from school he seemed restless, which surprised her. It had been the first sunny, warm day in about five months, and she had assumed the children would have had lots of fun on the playground during their two scheduled recess periods. But no. Her son explained that they hadn't been allowed outside. The teachers were worried that the kids might tell each other information that would affect their test performance. So these little nine- and ten-year-olds were kept inside on a beautiful day and given no time to run around or play, because it might cause trouble with the tests.

As schools scramble to ensure that children acquire measurable, marketable skills, they've turned their backs on one of the most important findings from the last hundred years of research in developmental psychology: that children need to play, and that play is essential to their future well-being.

In 2012 the school district in Syracuse, New York, chose to eliminate recess in order to make more time for children to learn "essential" academic skills. At the time Syracuse's student achievement, measured by statewide tests, was among the lowest in New York State. Chief academic officer Laura Kelley said, "If they are going to opt to do recess, they are going to be taking time from ELA [English language arts] and math, and that's a choice I hope every teacher considers very carefully."[8] She went on to explain to the reporter that instruction is more important than spending time on recess. And though there is a lively debate among scientists about the precise impact of various kinds of play on children's development, there is not much debate about the benefits of recess. Children behave better, experience (and exhibit) less stress, and enjoy better health when they have generous amounts of free time. In addition, a large body of research suggests that when children engage in various kinds of play they have opportunities to develop key intellectual abilities: the ability to take someone else's perspective, the ability to think about old problems in new ways, the ability to construct narratives, and the ability to negotiate with others, to name just a few. Once again, the unrelenting focus on using school as a means to creating employable adults has cost children dearly. A similar trend can be seen in the exclusion of art programs in schools. When schools are held accountable only for the accomplishments most obviously linked to future earnings, they sacrifice many of the experiences that are most important for optimal development but which are not lucrative.

The relentless focus on the bottom line has damaged schools in one other very important way: the carrot of money and the stick of unemployment discourage administrators, teachers, and children from taking risks. Last year I sat in on a sixth-grade science class in a suburb about forty-five minutes outside of New York City. The teacher was explaining to the children that the spring science fair was coming up and that it was time for them to figure out what their science projects would be. He began by telling them about some of the projects from the previous year. He pointed to one of the best, which was sitting on a shelf in the classroom. It was a glove with little lightbulbs on the tip of each finger. The label said it was a new kind of flashlight. The teacher explained that they too could invent something that would solve a problem (for instance, how to light your way in the night and still have two free hands, like the glove with lightbulbs). He pointed out that the glove was neatly made, clever, and useful. He told them exactly how much time they could spend on the project, and how they might budget their time to greatest effect. He explained the rubric the teachers would use to grade the projects. Then he suggested they get into small groups and begin figuring out what they wanted their projects to be.

I was sitting at one of the tables where children were talking. One twelve-year-old boy said, "I'm gonna make a battery. I've seen it done on YouTube. It's easy. I can do it in one weekend." Another boy said, "Yeah, that's cool. But I wanna invent something. I'm gonna invent a cake you can eat on a stick, like a lollipop. It'll be like the glove—funny and easy. I won't need a lot of materials." A third boy had been sitting quietly. When he spoke, his tone was slightly less certain, more speculative. "I wanna do something cool. I wonder if I could figure out how to do an experiment on animal behavior. I've always wanted to know whether crickets actually talk to each other when they make those noises."

The first boy piped up with a note of friendly caution: "You don't wanna do that, man. You're crazy. Where you gonna get the crickets? What if it doesn't work out?" The boy looked back at him, slightly embarrassed. "Yeah, you're right. I know. I can just build a cricket house instead. I saw a show about it. I think I have all the materials in the garage." In the space of two sentences the boy went from trying something interesting, ambitious, and worthwhile to a plan that assured him of moderate success. The teacher had, perhaps unwittingly, made it clear to the children that something clever and manageable was a better bet than something ambitious but uncertain and possibly unwieldy.

Children are discouraged, in ways both large and small, both subtle and obvious, from trying things at which they might fail:

reading difficult books, studying a complex topic, or taking a course that might lower their GPA. Why would a student try any of these things when she's been groomed to keep her eye on the prize of a good grade and the success to which it will lead?

The irony is that by encouraging children, however implicitly, to look for easy success, teachers and parents encourage what psychologist Carol Dweck calls "performance motivation."[9] Children lean toward the task that will allow them to shine rather than the task that will cause them to learn something new. Dweck explains that when children choose challenging tasks rather than easy ones, they are motivated by a desire for achievement (rather than shine, they prefer to get better at something or acquire new skills). So, in effect, when teachers encourage children to set their sights on a good grade, they are often indirectly encouraging children to shy away from the very challenges that will prove most educational.

Children aren't the only ones discouraged from pursuing interesting but uncertain avenues. Several years ago, a fourth-grade teacher came to me frustrated because her students seemed so reluctant to read except when they absolutely had to for a specific assignment. I asked the obvious first question: "What do they like to read?"

She looked taken aback. "What?" she said, staring at me.

"You know," I said, "maybe the problem is they don't have enough of the materials that really grab them. What grabs them?"

She looked uneasy. "I don't know. I spend so much time trying to make sure they have the reading skills they need, I don't really ask them what they'd like to read."

I said, "Well, why don't you spend a month letting them read whatever they want and see what happens? You won't know whether that will work if you don't try it."

As I was speaking, her face began to light up, and I could see her thinking about how to make that happen. "I could give them time after lunch to read what they want. I guess I could bring in some magazines and old books from my house for them. I guess I could invite them each to bring a book from their house that another kid in the class might like."

"Yeah," I said, "that sounds great."

Then a shadow fell over her face. "But a month is a long time." I could sense the window in her mind closing. "Maybe instead I should just encourage them to read at night. Make it clear that even though they have to read what I assign during class time, they are totally free to choose their own books after school." Experiment over, case closed. For a moment the teacher seemed eager to explore possibilities. But just as quickly she backed off, wary that such possibilities might get in the way of the mountain of very specific tasks and goals she felt she had to meet day in and day out.

She's not alone. Good, thoughtful teachers all across the country express a similar conflict: some of the innovations they'd love to try with their students just seem too risky. They know the usual methods aren't working, but they dare not deviate from the long list of demands made of them by administrators and policy makers. Though flexibility and a spirit of experimentation are essential to good teaching practices, there is nothing in the current system that encourages teachers to try out new methods and every reason for them to stay cautiously within familiar boundaries.

What's in the Pot of Gold?

Recently I was told about a thirteen-year-old boy named Ethan who lives with his mother and little sister on the West Coast. He had been shy in elementary school, but he was bright, he liked the other children, and he had teachers he felt comfortable with. Then after he finished fifth grade, it was time for him to move on to sixth grade in the much bigger middle school for his district.

The classes were boring, the halls were crowded, some kids were mean, and he couldn't get to know any of his teachers. He was miserable.

In October, though, he discovered something that made it all bearable: he learned that all of his work was graded and recorded online and that he could continually track his progress in each class, on several dimensions. Now each day he could log in and find out how he was doing. If learning wasn't fun, if school wasn't a happy place to be, at least he could find solace in a series of ever-changing numbers that, though fairly meaningless, gave him something to hang on to. His mother announced with a mixture of relief and bitterness that checking his scores online had become the only satisfying thing for Ethan about school.

An invisible hand has been guiding most of our educational decisions and practices. This hand has led us to labor under the burden of checking off endless lists of small skills and accomplishments, and securing good test scores. Children and teachers scurry to finish tasks quickly, leaving little time to pursue anything deeply. Superficiality has become a habit. The actual substance of a child's school day, the activities and interactions that unfold in the classroom and hallways, day in and day out, have increasingly become limited by marketability. The concern for future success in the market for jobs has replaced a quest to help children work at things they care about, get along with others, and discover what it takes to be informed and thoughtful about topics that matter to them.

THREE

Rich or Poor,
It's Good to Have Money

Every time I tell someone that the pursuit of money has warped our educational system and hurt our children, I see a shadow quickly come over that person's face. Whether I'm talking to a teacher, an economist, a psychologist, a political activist, or a parent, everyone's first, skeptical response is some version of the following: "You're not saying, are you, that money doesn't matter? Are you saying that it's okay for people to live in poverty? Schools lift people out of poverty! You couldn't possibly argue that that is not important." No, I couldn't argue that, because I'd be wrong, and I wouldn't argue that, because it would be despicable. But the paths that link schools, money, and happiness together are a little more complicated than most people think.

Money Matters

Years ago, I knew a woman in New York City who had taught for many years in the public school system. She used to say, "Rich or poor, it's good to have money." She was right. Money matters. I am not suggesting that schools should turn their noses up at the importance of a decent wage. Everyone needs money to achieve a reasonable standard of living. It's very hard to be fulfilled, happy, or productive if you live below the poverty line.

When people don't have enough money, they suffer in a range of very palpable ways, both physically and psychologically. Just to name some of the more obvious hazards, not being able to satisfy basic human needs such as food or shelter is so disruptive that it is nearly impossible for a person to function; moreover, uncertainty about where the next paycheck is coming from, how much food your family will have at the end of the week, or where you'll be living next month causes such profound stress that it can make an otherwise healthy person ill. The damage caused by poverty is perhaps greatest when it comes to children. Research has shown that children who live in extreme poverty not only suffer while they are young but also bear the marks of that poverty throughout their lives. The stress of the uncertainty, want, and instability associated with poverty has a direct effect on cognitive development. Children who do not have enough to eat, who are constantly moving to a new home, and whose parents are beside themselves with worry experience stress at an exponentially higher level than children whose families have some economic stability. When children live with chronic stress, their bodies produce hormones that inhibit neurological development.

We've known for almost fifty years that poor children are more likely to struggle in school. For many years we assumed that the link between poverty and low school achievement was because those children heard fewer words at home, had greater trouble attending school regularly, were less likely to have parents who could help them with homework, and were more likely to have poor health care. But we now know that the stress of poverty shapes their cognitive capacities at a very fundamental physiological level. Some of the effects are nearly impossible to overcome later. Poverty has a very long arm.[1]

Money and school are woven in a tight knot. While poverty puts children at academic risk, school attendance plays a crucial role in lifting people out of poverty. When all children in a nation can go to school, the country begins to do better in many ways.[2] Crime rates drop, violence between religious and ethnic groups is reduced, fewer babies die during their first year, life expectancy rises, and people enjoy better health. There is no question that in order to have a chance at a decent life, children must go to school. The data about this are unequivocal. Moreover, in our society, the number of years a child stays in school is important. The longer a student goes to school, the more likely he or she will be to get a job, keep a job, and earn a decent wage. Finishing high school is essential, and increasingly, going to college is key to getting a decent job, not only in the white-collar sector but also in the trades and in industry.

Recent research has shown that the quality of schooling matters as well. When teachers are knowledgeable, skillful, warm, and responsive, their students are more likely to stay in school long enough to get the economic advantage that school offers.[3] However, the link between schooling and economic advantage is only a piece of the puzzle. The bigger picture is more complicated.

Money Versus Happiness

Education is key to the well-being of a nation and an essential element in ensuring economic stability for individuals within a nation. But we have fallen into the trap of treating those facts as the whole story, believing that because money is essential it is also important. We treat marketability as the end goal of education. To be happy, one must have enough money for basic necessities and a certain amount of stability. But the idea that having more money means you'll be better off is just dead wrong.

Decades of research have shown that the amount of money people make does not correspond in any linear way with how happy they are.[4] In fact, some research has actually shown that there is a negative correlation between money and happiness, at both the personal and global levels. In 1995, economist Richard Easterlin debunked the prediction that if money makes people happy, then the wealthiest nations should be the happiest.[5] Using two well-established metrics, a nation's gross domestic product and an assessment of subjective well-being, he looked at the relationship between a country's wealth and the happiness of its citizens. His research included eleven nations (the United States, Japan, and nine countries in Europe) and concluded that happiness does not increase as a country's income rises.

In 2010 Easterlin extended this study to seventeen developing nations in Central and South America to examine whether that paradox still held in places where an increase in national wealth might be more dramatic. He used well-established surveys designed to find out how people think about their lives and what they feel about their circumstances, covering dimensions of urban life such as public transport, health care, education, immigration, job availability, affordable housing, and life satisfaction. He also included a financial satisfaction question: "How would you define, in general, the current economic situation of your family? Would you say it is 1 = very good, 2 = good, 3 = regular, 4 = bad, 5 = very bad?" As in his earlier research, Easterlin also tracked gross domestic product and measures of subjective well-being. He found that in not one of the countries he examined was there a significant relationship between the rate of economic growth and improvement in life satisfaction.

What would explain the counterintuitive finding that people who are living in a nation that is becoming richer do not become significantly happier? Research suggests that among the middle class, the more material wealth people have access to, the greater the stress they feel about their work, their religious values, and the decisions they make in day-to-day life. In one study, researchers asked college students how much value they placed on material wealth, the work they did, and religion.[6] In a second task the students were asked to respond to various scenarios that pitted these values against one another. For instance, in one scenario they had to say whether they'd rather have a boring, difficult job that paid well or an interesting, satisfying job that paid poorly. But this was not all. The researchers also assessed the level of conflict students felt over these choices. The data suggest that the more value a student placed on wealth, the more likely he or she was to feel serious levels of stress when making important life decisions.[7] In other words, the more you care about wealth, the more difficult you find it to navigate life's dilemmas.

One compelling explanation of this is that there is a disconnect between people's spending habits and the values they hold about family, community, religion, their occupation, and other meaningful parts of life. This creates a negative cycle between competition, materialism, and happiness. The belief that money makes us happy fuels competition, competition inspires materialism, materialism increases a fixation on money and a competitive drive, which leads to more materialism, and so on. Nowhere in this cycle is an opportunity for emotionally significant connections, engagement, or meaningful satisfaction that would lead to long-term well-being.

In another example of this negative cycle in action, researchers collected data in Singapore, a country with an extremely high per capita income and a large population of young people eager to make a great deal of money. The researchers asked ninety-two business students in their early twenties to rate the value society places on various life goals (e.g., being physically fit, enjoying parties, various kinds of luxury, a sense of security and safety, spirituality, fitting into society, achieving financial success). For each goal, participants were also asked to rate on a scale of 1 to 5 how likely it was that they would attain that goal. Then the students were asked to reveal the importance they personally placed on material wealth, a sense of well-being, lack of psychological distress, and overall personal happiness. Despite the fact that students' cultural and educational environment encouraged them to emphasize materialistic goals, the students who internalized those ideals the most (the ones whose ratings matched society's) suffered from the greatest amounts of distress and the lowest levels of well-being. These students were experiencing a kind of cognitive dissonance: what they were supposed to want did not match up with what they actually wanted. This led to self-doubt, low self-esteem, and insecurity.[8] When students are encouraged to seek money at the expense of other personal goals such as meaningful work or helping others, they rarely thrive. Though money is necessary, it is not sufficient for satisfying what psychologists now understand are the basic human needs.

In the mid-twentieth century, psychologist Abraham Maslow developed his classic theory of the hierarchy of needs.[9] By studying "exemplary people" such as Albert Einstein and Eleanor Roosevelt as well as the healthiest 1 percent of college students, Maslow came to the conclusion that humans have five specific areas of need. The first includes physiological needs, for air, food, sleep, water, sex, and homeostasis. The second is the need for safety, which is characterized by security of the body, employment, resources, morality, the family, health, and property. The third need is for love and belonging, expressed through friendships, family, and sexual intimacy. The fourth is the need for esteem: self-esteem, confidence, achievement, respect for others, and respect by others. The fifth is the most abstract and yet the most interesting: the need for self-actualization. This refers to the fulfillment of a person's full potential and includes the development of morality, creativity, spontaneity, problem-solving ability, lack of prejudice, and acceptance of facts. Maslow's theory has as much relevance now as it did in 1940. Yet our schools seem to function on the premise that once the basic needs are met, all else will follow. As long as schools can ensure that children will have jobs when they grow up, the higher levels of needs will be satisfied in due course. But that is not at all the case. Education can and should concern itself not with the lowest level of needs but with the highest.

Schooling once had lofty goals, but only for a limited population; as it expanded to reach a broader population, its goals became tightly intertwined with the labor market. This marriage of education and money rested on assumptions about the masses that were questionable at best. As the union of school and market unfolded, it carried with it premises (often unexamined) about what education is for. That's no less true today.

What happens in school should and can enable children to live thoughtful, satisfying, and meaningful lives. What students do, say, feel, think, and attempt each day should prepare them to create happy lives, not train them to work. Identifying better goals and meeting those goals at a much deeper level would make school more meaningful and, yes, more enjoyable for children and adults alike. Happiness is not a dirty word, and it's not icing on the cake. It should be the pot of gold at the end of the rainbow. It can be the goal of education.

FOUR

How Happiness Enriches Schools

Each September, roughly four million small children in this country step through the front door of a school building, wearing a backpack or carrying a small lunch box, and make their way into a kindergarten class for the very first time. Some have pigtails, some have cornrows, some have long silky brown hair, some have Mohawks, and some have buzz cuts. Some are wearing a tidy uniform, and others are wearing sweatpants and a dirty shirt. Some are wearing a brand-new sweater and LeBron James basketball sneakers, or a pretty dress and a sparkly headband; some are wearing faded hand-me-downs. Some of these children can already read; others don't get to eat breakfast. Whether they're pale- or brown-skinned, chubby-cheeked or wan, bouncing with cheerful energy or hanging back with trepidation, as each of these four million children step across the threshold and into the classroom, they step onto a path. But a path to what?

I have watched hundreds of mothers and fathers drop their small children off for the first day of kindergarten. In New York City, Los Angeles, or Boston, in Sheffield, Massachusetts, St. Ansgar, Iowa, or White Sulphur Springs, Montana, if you stop young parents in the park, on line at the grocery store, or in their kitchens and ask them what they hope for their child, they are not likely to say, "I hope he gets rich," "I hope she has a bigger salary than anyone else on her street," "I hope he becomes the boss," "I hope she has two cars," or "I hope he can buy any suit he wants." Most parents, no matter where their ancestors are from or what kind of work they do, will answer something like this: "I want her to be happy," "I want him to have a good life," or "I want him to find love." Though virtually all parents, whether they say it or not, hope their child will have enough money to live a decent life, money isn't what shapes their dreams. What does? Happiness.

Over a number of years, my students and I have asked more than three hundred parents what they dream of for their children. Some of the parents we have talked to work in banks, some in the IT industry. Some clean houses or weed gardens. Among them are secretaries, doctors, social workers, and musicians. Some spoke only English; others' first language was Spanish or Chinese. They live in Maine, New York, or Pennsylvania, Washington, New Mexico, or North Dakota. All those with a child twelve years old or younger say that what they want most is for their child to be happy. Not one mentions wealth, or even job success. When parents talk about their children's school experiences, they say things like "I want her to love learning," "I want him to know stuff," "I want her to learn about the world," and "I want her to find out what she's good at." I have never heard a parent say, "As long as she gets good test scores, I don't care what else she does," or "It doesn't matter what he learns, as long as it means he'll make money later on."

But when we ask parents of older children the same question, the picture shifts. The older the children, the more likely their parents are to mention money and job success. Many say things like "I want her to find work" or "I want him to get a decent job." Some are quite ambitious. One mother of a seventeen-year-old girl answered the whole survey with just a single two-word answer: "Med school."

It seems that the closer graduation looms, the more the students, teachers, and parents get backed into a narrower and narrower set of goals. As children move through the school system, people tend to give up on the idea that school can teach the abilities that underlie a good life. Expectations of what school can offer become shallower and more concrete. The idea that school can provide a student with a love of books, the ability to think in new ways, and a sense of purpose are replaced with the hope that school can get them into college, teach them a marketable skill, or prepare them for an AP class. And yet most parents can see, by looking at their own lives, that although a modicum of money is essential, in and of itself money can't make you happy. Going to school raises your chance of being gainfully employed. But once there, why not learn things that might actually help you lead a meaningful and satisfying life? What would it be like if happiness, rather than money, guided our educational process?

Pleasure Versus Happiness

Before saying another word about education, I need to clear up one common and unfortunate source of confusion. Let me begin with a little story about my own children. When my first son was three, he made a new friend at his nursery school, in Stockbridge, Massachusetts. We soon invited the little boy over to play. The two boys had a great time, building blocks, tearing around my house, having snacks, and enacting superhero dramas. The next day when it was time to pick the children up from nursery school, the little boy's mom, who would soon become one of my closest friends, said to me, "James had a wonderful time playing with Jake. He loved it over at your house. He asked me if we could play a game in which he would be Jake and I would act out the part of Jake's mother. When I asked what I needed to do to be you, he said, 'Oh, it's easy. All you have to do is keeping saying, "Here. Have a lollipop." ' " She smiled, and I couldn't tell if she was flattering me for being such a nice mom or letting me know she disapproved of how indulgent I had been. When my boys were little, I did think about what would make them happy. And like all those parents I've surveyed, I want that for them in the long run. But when it comes to children, there are at least two different kinds of happiness, and they lead to two different kinds of adulthood.

When people talk about happiness, what rushes to mind is the lollipop: momentary pleasure, often hedonistic, and sometimes bad for you. Even if the thought of temporary pleasures does not rub up against one's Puritan inclinations, the dangers of overemphasizing transitory pleasure in childhood are clear. Research shows that children who cannot delay pleasure are headed for all kinds of trouble—they are more likely to have substance abuse problems, do poorly in school, gamble, engage in reckless behavior, have difficulty overcoming obstacles, and fail to pursue long-term goals. While lollipops, television, and teasing may be pleasurable now and then, they don't lead to happiness. A school day in which you can do whatever you want, whenever you want, is certainly not the answer.

But there is a much more substantive kind of happiness, a form we actually know quite a bit about. Sure, I gave my boys sweets, lolled around on the couch with them watching James Bond movies, and let them spend hours playing hectic games of Beckon. But now that they are grown, when they talk about their childhood and the experiences that made them genuinely happy or put them on the path of happiness, their recollections have little to do with momentary pleasures. My eldest son recalls an assignment to read a biography and do a three-dimensional project demonstrating something about the book. For his project, he dressed his little brother as Sitting Bull and brought him to the class. He now says that was his first foray into performance art, which became a central aspect of his work. My middle son (the former Sitting Bull) recalls the time he led his scrappy baseball team, from his underdog school, to a victory over a bigger and wealthier school that they had never beaten before. My youngest son recalls planting a vegetable garden with his classmates.

My sons are not alone. When asked what makes them happy, most people think of things deeper and far more enduring than a lollipop, a fancy car, or a big bank account.

What do we know about the components of true happiness? Quite a lot, as it turns out. Philosophers such as Nel Noddings and Harry Brighouse and psychologists such as Martin Seligman and Daniel Gilbert offer a clear and vivid picture of what genuine happiness involves.[1] It includes engagement in meaningful activity, connection to other people, involvement in one's community, a sense of purpose and accomplishment, the ability to make one's own choices, and the capacity to feel joy.

Moreover, though the match between happiness in childhood and well-being in adulthood is not perfect, it's surprisingly good. For instance, children who are optimistic are more likely to be optimistic when they grow up. Children who interpret bad things as fixable and think they can change a situation or do better next time are likely to go on feeling that way as they get older. Children who have experienced the rewards of deep engagement are likely to seek out that experience again and again. Children who learn how to collaborate and compromise are likely to go on doing so and reap the benefits of community life. In other words, by making schools a place where children are happy, we can also teach them how to be happy adults.

Nor is this kind of happiness fuzzy or ephemeral. We have evidence that it is vital both to the individual and to society. In their important book *Mismeasuring Our Lives*, the economists Joseph E. Stiglitz, Amartya Sen, and Jean-Paul Fitoussi show that happiness is a much better indicator of a nation's well-being than standard economic indicators such as gross national product or gross national income.[2] Research psychologists will tell you that there are plenty of situations where it's a mistake to trust what people say about their own thoughts and motivations. For instance, people are notoriously wrong about what stereotypes they hold, why they chose their spouse, or how much work they did on a given day. On the other hand, people do seem to know how happy they are. The three economists point out that when it comes to happiness, what people say about how they feel matches up with more objective measures. People who report good life satisfaction (a sense of meaning and purpose, connectedness, interest in daily life, engagement in activities of some kind, and ability to experience joy) also visit the doctor's office less often, are more productive at work, and are less likely to get a divorce. Happiness is substantive, measurable, and very important.

Researchers often view children's happiness as an individual trait—the child who is optimistic, the child with an easygoing temperament, and the child with a strong self-concept. But even the sunniest child is more likely to flourish in some settings than in others. More important, many of the behaviors that lead to a happy adult life have less to do with one's personality and more to do with how one lives one's life. These habits and ways of doing things require cultivation. They don't come naturally. They must be learned. What if, instead of more tinkering, we reframed education? What if we made happiness the overarching goal of school? What would children need to learn in order to have a good chance of living a happy life?

Every term there comes a day when I ask the students in my

education course to spend a few minutes thinking about what they think all U.S. students should know or be able to do by the time they finish sixth grade and then by the time they complete twelfth grade. Then I ask them to call out items from their lists. I write these up on the blackboard, so that we have a group list. Even though the room is lined with huge blackboards, I invariably fill up all three walls and still cannot fit everyone's items up there. Initially, it seems like such an easy, intuitive task. At first students tend to say things like "Read. Do algebra. Understand the scientific method. Learn how to get along. Be familiar with U.S. history. Understand other cultures." Then they begin to fill in with the things at least some of them think are essential: "Balance a checkbook. Speak at least one other language. Use technology. Know how to work in groups. Study geometry. Fix a car. Write a good essay. Learn how to live healthily. Be familiar with various religions. Analyze a poem. Understand statistics. Become familiar with literature from around the globe. Appreciate nature. Learn public speaking skills. Learn how to teach something to someone else." The list goes on and on. I've rarely seen any item on that list that wasn't valuable, reasonable, and, for the most part, included in one form or another in our current educational standards. But, as my students also quickly realize, it's totally ridiculous. There is no way any school can ensure that a widely diverse group of students, in school six hours a day, five days a week, for nine months of the year, can learn all of these things in any meaningful depth. And there's no good reason why they should either.

Then comes the fun part of the class activity. We figure out which things are so important that without them a child would be stranded, but with them, she or he would be equipped to do all kinds of things later in life.

If the aim is to enable children to live happy lives, our list of goals should be short, so that educators can concentrate on making sure all children learn a few essential things very well. We'd dispense with the ever-growing list of ever more difficult demands that goes by the name "high standards" and replace it with the idea of depth: a few potent things learned so well that children could use them forever. Our list must consist of abilities that will enable all kinds of children to become all kinds of adults. We live in a diverse and complex society. Any educational system that assumes everyone will do similar kinds of work, read the same books, want the same luxuries, or live in the same kinds of neighborhoods is doomed to fail many of its students. We should discard the pointless expectation that everyone should learn the same information or academic skills. As I will show later, it's not that expertise and substantive knowledge are unimportant; it's just that they are a means to achieving a larger goal. School should provide all kinds of children—whether they are very smart or not, whether they come from a highly educated family or one in which they are the first to learn to read, whether they expect to be rich or strive simply for a decent wage, whether they live in the city or a rural area—with the tools for a happy life, which, as I will argue, includes expertise and knowledge.

I offer here a list of the eight dispositions that children can acquire in school and which, if learned well, would set children on the path to well-being.

Engagement

Centuries of writing from philosophers and theologians, as well as a wealth of recent research, have made it abundantly clear that one of the most important sources of happiness is immersion in a meaningful and complex activity, whether it's writing a book, fixing a car, improving one's golf stroke, cooking dinner, or planning a community gathering. Life is difficult and filled with pain, obligation, interruption, frustration, and drudgery, which means that getting deeply absorbed in something you love is easier said than done. It turns out that knowing how to find things you love to do and then throwing yourself into those activities often requires some effort and skill. Young children experience such immersion and full-out effort in everyday life. Just drop by the local park and watch the intensity with which children organize ball games, build a fort, or enact a game of superhero. However, once in school most children have few chances to figure out what they love and an equally slim opportunity to pursue it with any intensity. Typically, our schools have not focused on helping students build their capacity to identify what they love doing and to immerse themselves in it. But they could.

When my son played community basketball, in elementary and middle school, I not only watched his games but often would get there early and watch the practice before it ended. I had become captivated by the way the boys behaved in the gym, and by the way the coaches behaved as well.

On one rainy January day, I wandered into the community center in the small working-class town where the practices were held. There they were, fourteen boys in their ratty shorts and jerseys and their expensive sneakers. Like any group of boys who were twelve or thirteen years old, they were a motley crew. Some were five foot seven and had the first hint of facial hair. Others, small and childlike with high voices, looked like they still needed to hold someone's hand to cross the street. A few had haircuts and accents that revealed their privilege, maybe a doctor mom or a lawyer dad, and two of the children went to a nearby independent school. Most, however, had parents who worked in factories, mowed lawns, or cleaned houses. And since all but two went to the local schools, I knew something about how indifferent many of them were to school and how lackluster their academic performances were.

As I walked in, the coach, a sulky guy in his early forties who, when he wasn't coaching community youth basketball practices, worked as a roofer, was giving them instructions about how to break up into two teams to try a certain play. He barked at seven of them to take off their jerseys so that the kids would easily know who was playing on which side. The jerseys came off in an instant, revealing puny chests or chubby middles, with not a whisper of protest. Then he began shouting at them what to do. They raced into position, and as they started playing he began criticizing, correcting, and shouting some more. They stayed focused on the play, trying their best to do whatever he commanded. Then with a peremptory arm wave he shouted for the kids who were on the bench to sub for some of those who were on the court. The boys instantly obeyed. When the scrimmage was over, he pulled a few kids aside and told them in abrupt language what they needed to do differently. They nodded, focused completely on what he was saying. Finally, he told them all it was time to run "suicides," a basketball drill that involves running up and down the length of the court at top speed, over and over again. All fourteen boys rushed to line up at one end of the court and then began running, with him yelling at them to run faster. One ran so hard he threw up—and then began running again. When they were done, they seemed exhausted but ebullient, talking nonstop about basketball.

As I stood there in that dank gym with its ripe odor, listening to the thud of all those feet, a funny image came into my head. What would it be like to see all of those boys fling themselves with the same intense abandon, discipline, and focus into a reading lesson? What if a reading teacher walked into the classroom and said, "Now, get out those books," and sixteen children eagerly grabbed a novel, rushing to get to the page where they had left off? What if the teacher called out, "What was the author's intention with that paragraph?" and the children scrambled to have the best idea first? Over the years, that vivid apparition has come to me again and again, and along with the apparition comes a question: what would it take to funnel some of that natural inclination for effort and absorption into more intellectual work? The obvious and easy response is to lay out all of the reasons why basketball is different from reading (or math, or social studies, or science). But such thinking is a waste of time and misses the point. Of course there are reasons why learning to read will not be as naturally enticing or exciting or motivating as getting better at basketball. And it should go without saying that only certain children try out for basketball—they come to the gym with a liking for the game and an eagerness to do well. The same cannot be said of reading. However, reading teachers could learn something from the gym. The most important thing they can learn is this: almost all children have a natural yearning to fling themselves wholeheartedly into some effort. When that happens, there are two kinds of reward: the feeling of total exertion and immersion, and the accomplishments made possible through such effort.

The noted psychologist Mihaly Csikszentmihalyi described this intense experience as "flow"—a state in which people become unaware of time, feel as if they have merged in some way with the thing they are working on, and have a sense of total involvement with a particular activity.[3] Musicians, writers, furniture makers, cooks, and anyone solving an interesting problem that they willingly embarked upon know what flow feels like. It's worth noting that when Csikszentmihalyi described this kind of engagement in adolescence, he called it "negentropy"—the opposite of entropy. And he specified that negentropy involved constructive, socially meaningful pursuits. Getting high, dancing at a party, and drag racing, while perhaps absorbing, cannot lead to negentropy. Basketball, gardening, working on a play, debating, or solving mathematics problems, however, can involve negentropy. And according to a growing body of literature, such profound engagement is an essential part of optimal development

for children. Children who experience negentropy are more ener-
getic more of the time, try harder at various tasks, and generally
enjoy a greater sense of well-being than children whose days hold
little or no negentropy.

However, there is a second reason to make negentropy a central focus of K–12 education. Children who throw themselves
into an activity, who feel some sense of intrinsic motivation and
engagement, learn faster, learn more, and end up with greater expertise than children who do things simply because someone else
tells them it's worthwhile or because they are afraid of what will
happen if they don't do it. In recent years, Angela Duckworth has
urged researchers and educators alike to concentrate on what she
calls grit—purpose, effort, and engagement. Her research has
shown that self-discipline in middle school is a better predictor of
high school achievement than standardized test scores. In other
words, effort matters more than ability. However, not all effort is
the same.

The boys playing basketball were not just totally absorbed.
They were willing to undergo pain, frustration, and someone
yelling at them (including yelling criticisms), all so that they
could get better. And not one of them dropped out during the
season. In other words, they stuck with it. This combination of
absorption and what some call "stickiness" is key to well-being,
when you are young as well as when you are grown up. Why
not help children experience such stickiness not only so that
they will learn better and do more in school, but so that they
will seek such engagement in their adult lives? Teachers could
view such engagement as an educational goal rather than as the
nice but unessential grease that smoothes the way to some other
goal.

Some teachers do just this. At a small school in a suburb in
the eastern part of New York State, a teacher named Liz Bertsch
has a class in which children ages seven to eleven work together.

Twenty-five years ago, when Bertsch was in college, she majored in philosophy. She brings to her work with children an unabashed appetite for the intellectual and an expectation that they too have lively minds. All of her students, no matter what their age or background, read Chaucer, make three-dimensional models of the mind, and discuss the idea of infinity.

Years ago, I began working in her school, and I got to watch her teach. I saw that she came to class each day with wonderful ideas and armed with materials on challenging, engaging topics. But it seemed to me that even with such a great array of subject matter, the children seemed to downshift the minute Bertsch presented a new unit or topic of study. They instantly became just a little more passive and slightly disengaged. I could literally see them sit back a little in their chairs and slacken slightly, waiting to be told what would happen and what they should do next. It dawned on me that no topic, regardless of how lively its presentation, would elicit the kind of intense effort and involvement children are capable of when they have some choice in what they do and some investment in the outcome (other than a grade). On the other hand, when children do work that really matters, either because they care so much about it or because it will have a real impact on others, they involve themselves on a whole other level. It could be winning a basketball game, writing something others will read, or cooking something others will eat. When children know their efforts will be used, seen, or savored by others, arbitrary rewards become irrelevant—the work provides its own powerful incentive to excellence. I proposed to Bertsch and some of her fellow teachers that they rethink their classrooms. Instead of planning a series of projects and activities designed to "cover" topics or subject, why not think about a few complex and ambitious endeavors—things that would require all kinds of intellectual and physical industry and that would demand real creativity and problem solving? And instead of ending with a demonstration of what the children had learned, all this industry would result in work that would affect others in some way. I suggested that instead of *subjects* they think of *endeavors*.

After just a few days, Bertsch announced to me that she had always wanted to make films, and thought her students might also. She explained that making films would require all kinds of work and present the children with interesting intellectual challenges. She was going to devote considerable time to helping them make short films, individually or in small teams. Two months later, she announced that they would hold a film festival and invite the community to a public screening. As she described her process:

> We made a film titled *Mustache*. I had decided that it would be a lot easier to begin making a film with kids if we made silent films for the first year, and so we watched a lot of Chaplin and some Buster Keaton. They loved Chaplin. We decided that having a mustache would be immediately funny and so we developed, as a class, a narrative around a mustache. As a group, we composed the following plot. A magic potion is discovered by a person digging in the ground. On the label is the word "mustache," and so the person (an eleven-year-old boy) rubs it on his lip. When he awakens the next morning, he is wearing a very impressive mustache. He shares his potion with many friends, and some sprout a mustache and others do not. Those who did not sprout a mustache are furious; feeling tricked, they start a war with those with the mustaches. It involved a very dramatic swordfight on the hill behind the school, and we decided that it needed a musical montage, so we added the Rolling Stones' "Gimme Shelter." Everyone goes down during the battle except for the person who originally found the bottle. He decides to rebury the potion—and then the film fades to black.

The film was a great hit. More important, the children involved worked night and day. First they spent days discussing the role of action in a narrative. They argued about what makes something a good story. They analyzed a series of texts (in film and literature) to figure out the difference between funny dialogue and funny gestures. They talked about what makes an ending work well. They wrote and rewrote the script. They learned how to use a camera, and why the position of the camera changes the story; in other words, they learned about perspective. They learned how to edit, and talked about the role of editing in creating good work. They rehearsed. They argued about specific segments of the film that didn't seem to work. All told, they learned how a fine piece of work is put together, and how to identify the components of a narrative. They talked about the meanings the audience might take from their film. They discovered the role of music in shaping the audience's reaction.

Three years later, one of the boys, now eleven, decided the group should make a film called *Mustache 2*. Clearly, the project had remained in his mind, not just as a memory but also as something to think about. What more could you ask for from an academic lesson?

A close look at what went into making *Mustache* shows how deeply engaged the children were in complex and academically important issues. In fact, they wrestled with the very problems we consider seminal to what it means to be literate. But they did it with an intensity and commitment rarely triggered by a five-paragraph essay. This shouldn't surprise anyone. In Ann Brown's seminal research, conducted in the 1980s and 1990s, she showed that when children have control over what they are learning and how they are learning it (what Jerome Bruner calls "agency"), they learn more thoroughly and remain more interested in the material.[4] The mistake educators have often made is thinking that they have to choose between getting students engaged and helping their students learn important valuable material. But actually, the two can easily go together. The title of Ann Brown's work on this subject embodies this conviction: "Creating a Community of Learners About Things That Matter."[5] In one of her studies, children worked in small groups to understand how animals created their habitats. Her goal was for them to learn how to think like and work like biologists, but to do so in ways that absorbed them fully. They didn't learn about biology. They constructed biological knowledge. The point is that the topic, whether Charlie Chaplin or sea turtles, doesn't matter as long as the underlying intellectual skills are foundational and important. However, this works only when children are given a chance to learn those intellectual skills in the service of doing something they find deeply and fully absorbing.

But Bertsch knew that what would absorb one group might not fit another. If knowledge is really constructed, not digested, then each group must construct knowledge that is compelling to it. So several years later she found her class doing a whole different thing:

> We just produced a performance of *A History of the English Language*. The older kids researched how English developed from the times of the Roman occupation of the British Isles up until about the 1400s, then composed their research into a performable script in which the younger kids acted out all of the major battles, concluding with the Battle of Agincourt as they recited text from Shakespeare's *Henry V.*

In other words, engagement is not opposed to intellectual rigor. It makes such rigor possible.

Some years ago, I visited a public high school situated on the Lower East Side of New York City. This particular school was on the third floor of a ratty building that looked nothing like a school on the outside. Several other small public schools took up the other floors. The school was designed for students who were on the verge of dropping out (or being expelled). These were kids who had a steady record of failing grades, had gotten into trouble with the law, had become addicted to drugs and alcohol, or had become pregnant. This was a last-chance school for last-chance kids.

I saw some of the kids shuffling along, as only teenagers can do, lounging as if there were no reason to rush to class. Peeking into one classroom, I saw one pretty girl sitting straight and focused on the teacher, several long-limbed boys with their legs stretched out and looking as if they were considering ordering a beer but might listen to the teacher instead, and a few kids laughing with one another—exactly what you might expect looking into a classroom with unusually devoted teachers, an excellent principal, and a somewhat difficult group of students. But then I passed a classroom where all of the kids were hunched forward looking at one another intensely and all you could hear was the sound of the person speaking. I stepped inside.

Eleven of these last-chance students were talking about the First Amendment: how it affected their lives and whether there were any exceptions to free speech. One tall, skinny boy whose waistband hung halfway down his backside began to speak. His voice was quiet and intense. "I was arrested last week. I was so angry. That guy wouldn't let me talk. I wanted to explain why I jumped the turnstile. I guess I cursed. But he didn't give me a chance to talk. I was trying to tell him he was biased against me. He said I should shut up. Now I've read this thing [the First Amendment], I wonder." He went on to explain his new ideas to the group, which listened and reconsidered previous opinions. Periodically the teacher provided some history or context about the First Amendment. At one point she suggested an angle they hadn't thought of. In class after class I had seen kids looking out the window or down at their cuticles. I had seen them interrupt one another as if they couldn't care less that other people were speaking. But here in this classroom, talking about the Constitution and its impact on them, they spoke as if their lives depended on figuring it out. They sat there talking, without distraction, disruption, or disengagement, for almost an hour, till the end of class, and then stayed halfway through their lunch period. When at last they had to go, they asked the teacher if they could continue the discussion the next day.

We teachers have tended to think that if we can make an uninteresting topic or activity appealing to students, they will learn it. Using this mind-set, the problem becomes "How can I make the Constitution seem fun?" or "What activity can I do to make learning the mechanics of good literature more like a game?" It's the spoonful-of-sugar approach to education.

This can seem like it's working, and often it has. You trick kids into learning what you want them to learn. But the spoonful-of-sugar approach robs students of the chance to practice real engagement, which ultimately is much more important than their knowledge of the Constitution. Anyone can learn about the First Amendment anytime. But acquiring the habit of sustained engagement is best learned in childhood. If we made engagement the priority, rather than using it as a nice trick to get kids to learn what we want them to learn, we'd be teaching them something they really would use later in life.

Purpose

When I first met the *New York Times* columnist Thomas L. Friedman, two things about him surprised me: he was shorter than I expected, and sunnier. I had never seen him on TV, but having read his books and columns and felt a sense of authority and drive spitting from every piece, I expected a larger man. I was also struck by how ebullient he seemed. The seriousness of his topics and the certainty with which he expressed his views had not prepared me for his cheeriness. Love him or hate him, most readers acknowledge that he's had a tremendous impact on the way people across the world think about global politics. No one could deny that he's been remarkably productive and successful. Among other things, he's won three Pulitzer Prizes. It began to occur to me that his drive and ebullience came, at least in part, from his enormous sense of purpose. As he has said, "I still can't wait to get up every morning, put my pants on, and go to work."

We know that people are born with differing levels of drive. Clearly Friedman was born with bucketfuls, and his successes have only fed that drive. But one need not be Tom Friedman to be lifted up and forward by the feeling that one's life has a purpose. Recently I attended an Alcoholics Anonymous meeting to help a loved one celebrate an anniversary of sobriety. A man named Frank was hosting the meeting. Frank was in his late seventies, with snow-white hair and a weathered face, his cheeks bright red from having worked outdoors in the late March sun and wind. I learned at the meeting that Frank had been sober for more than forty-five years. But as a young man he had been such a serious drunk he had lived on the streets for three years. After getting sober, he moved to a rural town on the East Coast, where he became an electrician and a father to five. He also became a pillar of the sober community. At the end of the meeting, I learned that he suffers from a terminal illness, has an infirm wife, and many years ago lost a child to cancer. But when I asked his friends from AA whether he is sad, the answer was instant and unanimous: "Oh, no. Not sad. He's filled with joy and so much energy still. He feels there's so much left to do." It seems he too cannot wait to get his pants on every morning.

In his famous description of the psychosocial stages of human development, Erik Erikson comes back, time and again, to the idea that a sense of place in the world is central to human well-being. According to Erikson, it's not enough to have a good relationship with your parents, to feel confident, or even to satisfy your most basic drives. Optimal development depends on feeling connected to society.[6] Moreover, connection in Erikson's scheme doesn't just mean feeling included in one's community. It means making a meaningful contribution. A look at the stages he identified makes this apparent. The four-year-old is caught between a sense of inferiority and industry, while the aging adult veers toward generativity or stagnation. Both young and old need to feel that what they do matters.

As people know who've thrown themselves into something that felt really significant (a political cause, an effort to raise money for a neighbor, making art, solving a crime, or helping those in need), boring work, long days, and frustrating setbacks are insignificant when you have a sense that what you are doing matters, that you have a goal worth struggling for. In contrast, even people fortunate enough to have great ease and good luck report a sense of emptiness and dissatisfaction when they lack meaningful goals. Research has shown that a sense of purpose is key to life satisfaction.[7] For some, that purpose is the work itself (the novel written, the house built, the patients healed, the students taught), but to be honest, not everyone finds an inherent sense of purpose in their work. If you are employed in a gas station, on an assembly line, or on a factory farm, your work is not likely to bring you this all-important sense of purpose. And yet everyone is entitled to such a sense, and everyone should be able to find it in some regular part of life, whether it's through community service, caring for family, or making art.

One of the most remarkable things about children is their capacity for industry. Watch any child try to take apart an old clock, build a fortress, or invent the rules of a new game, and you will see a level of focus, enthusiasm, and effort that most of us would give our eyeteeth to experience in our jobs. It's hard to get in the way of children who are intent upon making something, taking something apart, or figuring something out when it is meaningful to them.

While most three-year-olds in our culture are, by design or benign neglect, given lots of time to delve into things that feel meaningful to them (learning the names of animals, finding out why ice cubes melt, creating a baseball diamond in a back lot), once they get to school, their own sense of meaning and purpose is put on a twelve-year hold. What if, instead, school was a place where children built up their sense of purpose, learned how to identify their own goals, and acquired ways to meet those goals? For this to be genuine, children would need at least some opportunities during the school day to actually make choices and come up with their own plans.

Ironically, in the nineteenth and early twentieth centuries, when schools played a smaller part in children's lives, at least some had greater opportunities to stumble upon, or cobble together, their own goals. When winter came, my stepfather, a potato farmer on eastern Long Island, used to skip school for weeks at a time in order to go duck and goose hunting with his buddies, the sons of other farmers. Sometimes the school principal would join them. And once planting season began in April, he and his friends were done with classes for the year. Back in the 1930s in rural America, school was only one part of what young people did to prepare for adult life. Many children then had more chances to feel a sense of purpose, if not in school, then in life more generally. Andrew Carnegie describes the thrill of knowing that his work, first in a cotton factory and then in a telegraph office, helped his family survive. Ironically, when adults began to protect childhood via labor laws and by emphasizing what were termed "developmentally appropriate practices," we went too far. Schools have become so focused on advancing children's skills for the future there is little thought given to whether the children feel useful in the present.

And yet when children work toward goals that really matter to them, their capacity to learn multiplies. This idea isn't exactly new—John Dewey argued for something similar more than a hundred years ago. Sad to say, most educators who think at all about John Dewey take what he said to mean that children's schoolwork should feel relevant. But as my former student Hannah Hausman says in talking about math education, "There is a difference between realistic and real." A math problem that concerns skateboards or popular music may seem like it will be more interesting and appealing to kids than a problem that is about apples or bricks. But it will work only in the most transitory and superficial sense. A teacher who suggests that children can plan pretend menus as a way of learning how to calculate money isn't really changing anything. Having teachers set up pretend scenarios robs a child of her own play and keeps her outside the loop of real life. What if, instead, children were given some opportunity to really think about what they wanted to make, investigate, or do? What if teachers asked children to make things that actually had an impact on the lives of others, whether preparing food, writing books for other children to read, creating math games for others to play, sewing quilts, or building sheds?

In the 1930s, when Oklahoma was as dry as a bone, weary and hungry farm families made their way to California, in desperate search of work. But there was none to be found. Many died of hunger, illness, and futility. In 1937 the federal government created a series of camps where these migrant workers could take shelter and receive some help. However, when the families tried to send their children to the local schools in the area, the children were faced with ridicule, exclusion, and discrimination. They were poor, they were in bad health, many had never received any schooling at all, and they were clearly different from the local children. A savior arrived in the form of an educator named Leo Hart, who convinced the local schools to give him the money that by law they would have to spend on the Okie children attending their schools. Hart used the money to create a community school right in the midst of the Weedpatch Camp.[8] He hired some new teachers from other places, and no matter what their degrees or areas of expertise, each was asked to wear many hats. Lee Hanson, for instance, agreed to teach English, plumbing, electrical wiring, sports, and aircraft mechanics. Some of the teachers helped out in the cafeteria. The first two years, the students in the Weedpatch School helped construct their own schoolhouse. They also studied things like English, typing, and science. When you read accounts of the experience, it is clear that everything these children and their teachers did was infused with a sense of a purpose far more meaningful than a grade at the end of the day. They were creating something together that they all needed and wanted. The students of the Weedpatch School went on to become store owners, teachers, school principals, businessmen, and even a judge.

Years ago, a teacher I was helping came to talk to me, holding a piece of paper on which he had listed some goals he had in mind for his students that year. "First of all," he said, "I know they need to do some math. Some of them just need to get better at adding and subtracting. But others are ready for some geometry, and for making complicated calculations. They all need to learn something about proportions. But that's not all. I want them to learn how to plan. They just sit there waiting for the next piece of work. They seem clueless about how to take an idea and make it a reality, step by step. That's not something I can tell them. They have to go through it themselves." But his list didn't end there. He wanted them to work together. And he wanted them to be confronted by real problems that needed real solutions. He also wanted them to do more independent reading. Another teacher might have figured out a series of activities or lessons targeted for each of those goals: reading time each day, math worksheets, and regular puzzles or conundrums to solve. But this young teacher took a different approach. He gathered his students into a circle and began talking to them about the problem of reading. What was keeping them from spending more time with their books? They said there were no comfortable seats and no good spots in the room for reading. They explained to him that when they read for fun, they liked a cozy corner or a place where they could sprawl. Some of them said that they liked to get away from all the busy sounds of work in order to get lost in a book. This made sense to him. He preferred to read in bed, but as a child had liked lying underneath the kitchen table.

What, he asked the group, could they do? Make a reading corner in the room? They measured the room. They discussed the other things that needed to happen each day in their class. They quickly realized there wasn't enough space to dedicate some to a reading corner. "Let's not stop there," he urged. "Let's figure out a solution." Bent forward eagerly in the circle, increasingly caught up in the challenge of finding a way to read in the classroom, they both talked and listened, making sure they didn't miss the good idea someone else might suggest. Together, they wound their way toward the good idea: a reading loft. As documented in a journal one of the children kept about their efforts, they spent weeks designing the loft, trying to figure out how to make it nice, how to lift it above the fray of the classroom, how to make sure it didn't intrude on the space below. They made designs. They asked a parent in the building business to come look at their design. They ordered the materials, figuring out along the way what they would have to spend out of the budget allotted to their classroom, and what they might not be able to buy later in the year as a result. And finally, months later, they had built themselves a reading loft.

During that time the students ended up learning something about each of the things their teacher had originally listed (math, planning, reading, collaboration). They came to school each day restless to get back to building the loft. Most important, they had the chance to work hard and learn new things for something that mattered to them, something that gave their work meaning and purpose.

Curiosity

One of the most remarkable characteristics of young children is that they have a nearly unquenchable thirst for knowledge. It helps explain why they are such efficient and powerful learning machines. But, as research has shown, this natural curiosity dwindles over time.[9] By the time they are in sixth grade, children show almost no curiosity when they are at school. The easy explanation is that curiosity is just one of those characteristics that naturally wanes with age, like uproarious laughter or a love of candy. But actually, that is not the case. The reason curiosity wanes is that we don't nurture it.

I have never been in a conversation about education, whether with businesspeople, academics, principals, schoolteachers, or parents, where they didn't go on and on about how important it is for children to love learning. They're right. Our urge to find out is what leads us to learn, and it makes life interesting. It is also the most influential factor across all sorts of entrepreneurial activity. Many students who will never take to academic learning in a formal classroom sense—and thus will never become doctors or lawyers—have the potential to become great entrepreneurs. But even if a person is not destined to start a business or invent something important, an appetite for knowledge is what fuels progress at every level. Not only that, but children learn more easily when they are curious about the material to be learned. Yet for all the talk about a love of learning, few schools do anything deliberate to foster curiosity. It is one of the great untapped psychological resources for learning, and key to an enriched adult life.

Though babies are born with a tremendous urge to find out, that urge becomes increasingly fragile over time. Without the right support and guidance, most children's appetite for knowledge dwindles rapidly between the ages of four and eighteen. This may explain why the majority of students in this country report a feeling of boredom and disengagement in school. The irony, of course, is that curiosity is the single most powerful ingredient of learning. The best way to help people learn is to tap into their curiosity. Watch anybody try to learn something they actually want to know; little can stop them. Research shows that when somebody's curiosity is piqued (whether it concerns who is getting a divorce, how a flashlight works, what ants eat, or who was responsible for Watergate), their understanding is deeper and their memory for the information lasts longer. And yet once again we treat this curiosity as a deal sweetener rather than the real deal.

Years ago, I watched a group of fourth graders in a science class. The teacher was explaining that the students were to form small groups and work on an activity to learn about how the ancient Egyptians had first invented wheels for transport in order to carry stones for their huge pyramids. She then organized the children into groups of three and invited each group to come up and get the materials they needed—a flat piece of wood with a metal eye at one end, some round wooden dowels, and a small measurement device that records the amount of force required to pull an object at a given speed for a given distance. The device had a string with a hook attached to it so that children could hitch it to the bar. She also gave each group a worksheet to fill out, which included step-by-step instructions about what to do with the materials and a series of questions. Each group was to try pulling the wood piece along the floor, measuring how easily they could drag it both with and without dowels underneath it. By this time, it had become clear to me that the idea was for each group to "discover" that pulling the board was a lot easier with the dowels serving as wheels.

The children happily sorted into their assigned groups, materials in hand, and found a space on the floor to settle down and work. As they began completing the steps outlined on the worksheet, the noise level rose. The teacher wandered around, looking down on the groups from above, encouraging, giving tips, and reminding them to answer the questions on the worksheet. Several times she noted that they were "moving right along," "making good progress," or "getting there." I looked around the room to see who was pulling the wooden bar, who was recording the measurements, and who was watching quietly. Then I noticed one group that seemed to have forgotten the worksheet and was instead intrigued by the equipment. The children were trying to figure out different ways to use the bar with the spring scale attached—yanking, pulling, and even at one point holding the string up high so that the bar was simply swinging in the air, hanging from the device. Then they stood the dowels up like columns and tried to balance the bar on the dowels. Finally, they tried surfing the bar along the surface of the dowels, which they had laid down to create something like a conveyer belt. At this point, the teacher also noticed what they were doing. She called out to the group, over the heads of the other students, in a loud clear voice for all to hear, "Okay, kids, enough of that. I'll give you time to experiment at recess. This is time for science."[10]

It is certainly possible that some of the children took away a wonderful lesson about how the Egyptians discovered wheels. It is also likely they learned something about measuring the relationship between force, speed, and distance. But the overarching thing they were learning was how to follow instructions in a timely way. However, had the teacher shifted the activity just a little bit, they might have learned quite a bit about how to form a question and how to seek an answer. This skill is likely to be much more powerful in the long run than knowing how wheels were invented. It wouldn't have taken all that much for the teacher to shift the focus: she might simply have offered her students the same materials, given them some time to play with the materials, and then asked them to identify a question that using the materials would answer.

I have seen this work well. In one elementary school I know, children spend time each day in the science lab. The teacher conducts several experiments that interest her (she is pursuing a graduate degree in biology). The children are invited to help on her projects. But at some point she begins asking them what they want to know about the natural world. Her plan is to get them engaged in original research. Figuring out what is a good question is a priority. The scientific idea of a good question is quite specific—a question that can be answered with data. It's remarkable how few people understand the process by which a broad question becomes a scientific question, and how you get from there to a method for finding an answer. If children were given a chance to pursue what interested them, they'd be likely to absorb lessons in scientific method with alacrity. We currently focus on teaching children scientific information, though we should be teaching them how to inquire as scientists.

Thoughtfulness

When my son Sam was in high school he used to come home and say, "Oh yeah. I got the 'but still' argument again in class." The "but still" scenarios always began the same way. Someone would make an assertion ("War is necessary," "Two hundred feet is longer than seventy meters," "X does not equal Y," "The civil rights movement changed nothing," "Marijuana should be legal"), and another person would present compelling evidence that the first speaker was wrong. The first speaker would stare for a moment, temporarily stymied by the information, and then say, "Yeah, but still . . . ," and proceed to press on with his or her own point of view. That kind of response is funny now and then. But social psychologists describe this as a general social phenomenon, one that helps account for the irrationality of many of our decisions. In general, people find it hard to use evidence to guide their thoughts, decisions, and actions. And yet this is supposed to be the key feature of the educated person. Aristotle described the educated person as someone able to entertain an idea thoroughly without accepting it. The Nobel laureate Daniel Kahneman and a legion of other cognitive and social psychologists have shown that human beings are capable of slow, careful deliberation. Equally crucial is that people can base their beliefs on evidence. But these dispositions do not come easily or naturally to most of us; they're a product of the educational process.

And the data show that we're not doing a very good job of teaching our students how to think this way before they get to college. Andrew Shtulman asked college freshmen whether they believed in various invisible entities (such as God, the tooth fairy, and spirits).[11] He also asked them how confident they were that others thought the way they did, and to articulate their reasons for believing or not believing in each entity. It turns out that these students, all of whom had completed twelve years of schooling in the United States, all smart enough and motivated enough to get into good colleges, made no distinction between what they believed and what they knew based on evidence. In other words, they had made it through our whole K–12 educational system and still had no appreciation for the unique power of evidence.

If there is one thing most people pay lip service to when they talk about education, it's the importance of what many call "critical thinking." Public or private, urban or rural, conservative or liberal, most educated people will say that children should learn how to think in school. And they're right. Thinking is something you can get better at. Just as significant is that it's something others can help you learn. And yet we have done little in schools to help children think well.

Part of this may be an inevitable, if unfortunate, result of the explosion of research in psychology that has taken place over the last fifty years. In the 1960s and 1970s psychologists began to explore the inner workings of children's minds in a whole new way. The psychologist Jean Piaget had shown that the right questions or tasks could lead children to reveal not only what they were thinking but also how they were putting together information and what their reasoning was. Meanwhile, researchers began to realize that the computer offered a model of the human mind, one that led to all kinds of clever experiments about how children acquired knowledge and built up their understanding. It was an exciting time to study children's minds. Fifty years' worth of experiments later, we know lots and lots of very specific things about very specific processes: what happens when a child who has trouble matching sounds and letters practices targeted techniques, how children's understanding of living things can be elicited at an earlier age than we thought, and what you can do to temporarily enhance a child's ability to reason about abstract entities. Taken together, this vast sea of findings has moved us forward in our model of the developing mind. But it hasn't helped our schools all that much. In fact, all of these somewhat compartmentalized and atomized findings have fragmented curricula and teaching in such a way that children may spend a lot of time learning the supposed components of thinking without being given much time or encouragement to *actually think*.

Let me give one tiny example that would be hilarious if it

weren't tragic. Several years ago, I was collecting data on children's curiosity in a public school. I was sitting in the corner of a kindergarten room watching the children choose their seats for snack time. The teacher and her helpers had set out crackers, small squares of cheese, and little cups of juice. The children were, as usual, happy for snack time, filled with cheerful energy, and chatty. Then the teacher announced that today she would let the children tell jokes at recess, a periodic treat she offered them. She reminded them that to tell a joke a child would have to raise his or her hand and be called on, and then also reminded the other children to listen politely. They wriggled with pleasure. And then, just before the festivities commenced, she reminded them, with a stern look of warning on her face, "Remember boys and girls, this is the time to tell real jokes. Do *not* make any up yourself. Today we're only telling real ones."

On the face of it, this rule seems harmless enough, but it actually contains a damaging message. Making up jokes requires careful and often complex thinking, whereas telling "real" ones does not (it requires other good things, such as timing and showmanship). But the suggestion implicit in her warning, that making jokes up was somehow naughty or a waste of time, was just one more example of the way in which our schools fail to encourage the very thing we should most want our students to learn: how to think.

How well a child thinks depends on several factors, only some of which a teacher or school can influence. For one thing, children vary in how intelligent they are. All other things being equal, the smarter child will be able to take in more information at a faster rate, enabling her to think in more complex, flexible, and informed ways than the child who is less intelligent. Similarly, children who read a lot are likely to have certain intellectual habits that make them better thinkers. For instance, they're more able to think at an abstract level, more able to consider ideas and experiences that are somewhat foreign to them, and more able to construct and evaluate ideas that include information and reasons. However, even a child who is of average intelligence (and by definition that includes most children) or the one who isn't an avid reader can become better at thinking.

Teaching children how to think can be accomplished in many ways. Children can be encouraged to develop ideas by expanding on their hunches, questioning their intuitions, looking for evidence to back up their claims, and testing their ideas against evidence. They also can be asked to answer questions about their ideas and, just as important, to revise their ideas in the face of good arguments or new evidence. This process, straightforward as it may seem, is almost completely absent from most schools. Of course, it only works if a child is asked to develop an idea she actually cares about and finds interesting; to expect otherwise would be like asking someone to write a good novel using a plot she cares nothing about.

The philosopher Harry Brighouse has suggested that one of the most important things children can get out of school is the ability to think about something in a sustained way for twenty minutes. This is one of the most compelling educational proposals I've heard of in a very long time. His suggestion, though phrased in such a simple and concrete way, captures the powerful idea that good thoughts take time, and that the ability to spend time considering a thought is essential. There is no way to learn how to think something through, slowly and open-mindedly, except to do it.

To be thoughtful is to spend time examining an idea—testing its internal logic, weighing evidence, imagining how the idea might play out in everyday life, considering its opposite, and speculating about variations on the idea. It calls for a willingness to embrace ideas that might make one slightly uncomfortable.

Thoughtfulness requires skill, but it also depends on a mind-set—the sense that being thoughtful is worthwhile and a pleasure.

If students spent time and energy developing ideas, and if they use evidence as the cornerstone of those ideas, they would be in a much better position to make good decisions for themselves and others, to solve problems both at work and at home, and to participate in reasoned exchanges within their communities.

Mastery

When I met Mitch, he was a scruffy freshman in high school, on the verge of dropping out. His mouth was narrow and twisted with discomfort, and he had trouble looking adults in the eye. He was failing most of his classes, and he hated them. He felt school had nothing for him. Looking back, he said, "I didn't care much. I guess you could say I was a troublemaker. I was always late to classes. I was getting bad grades. I didn't care. As long as I got out of here." Then several friends and a guidance counselor suggested to him that he sign up for a project some kids within his school were starting. It was going to be a school within the school, run by students, for students. Mitch admits that he was so turned off by learning and schools that when he heard about the project, he thought, "I'm not doing this; it's lame. Why bother?" But given the alternatives, he figured he had nothing to lose, so he signed up.

As part of the plan, he was asked to think of something he really wanted to learn, and then work out how he could become good at it. With the help of the counselor and the other students in the group, he made a plan. He would spend half of each school week for the next three months devoting himself to this endeavor. He had always wanted to cook, he said. He liked to be around food. He had a feeling he might be good at it if he tried. He set up an apprenticeship with the chef of a local top-notch restaurant.

When he was back in the school building, he used the kitchen that was part of the home economics program to practice the new techniques he had seen. Meanwhile, he continued reading, writing, and doing various kinds of research with the other students in his experimental program. He learned to cook well enough to serve a five-course meal to over a hundred people at the end of the term. The restaurant where he had interned hired him as a regular sous chef. But what he said about the experience is just as important: "I feel more confident about myself. I can gather information on my own, learn things on my own. I know it. I know that I know it. And I know that I can express myself through it."

Mitch is not alone. Everyone yearns to be good at things. Abundant research shows how important such mastery is to a sense of well-being.

In the 1980s and 1990s a flurry of research suggested that when people felt good about themselves, they functioned at a much higher level. It was assumed that self-esteem made you try harder at things, made you kinder to others, and generally turned you into a healthier person. During the heyday of its popularity, self-esteem became one of the linchpins of a good childhood. You could hear parents and teachers talking about self-esteem as if it were a bodily fluid: "Her self-esteem is down; that's why she's not doing her math," or "Look how much we've raised his self-esteem; he's a much happier kid now."

However, researchers soon began to find that self-esteem was not a unitary dimension. You can feel confident and good about one aspect of yourself, but somewhat shaky about another. Then researchers began to find that in some cases, when children—or adults, for that matter—felt too puffed up about themselves, they actually behaved worse. For instance, when experimenters raised a child's confidence about his or her worth and capabilities (giving subjects false feedback about how well they had done on a video game or a school task), the children were more likely to act aggressively toward a peer who they thought had been mean to them. In other words, children with high self-esteem lash out more easily at others. Finally, it turned out that telling a child he is good at something doesn't lead to the same kind of self-worth as making sure he really is good at something. The answer, it turns out, is not to give children lots of empty praise but to ensure that each child has a chance to experience mastery.

When children become good at something, they are much more likely to invest future effort in it. They also begin to have a sense of what mastery feels like, so when they enter a new realm, they are equipped to seek mastery again. Studies show that children who are encouraged to think about their own learning learn more, but they also can apply those skills in a new domain. When children have a sense of their own agency and can reflect on and evaluate what they have learned, they have "learned how to learn." Though this phrase has become so ubiquitous as to be trite, there is a real meaning to it, with psychological research to back it up. Why shouldn't we make the experience of mastery a goal of our system? If mastery itself were the goal, rather than mastery of a certain topic, schools would be much freer to pick the domains that really engaged students, and therefore much more likely to lead more children to a more authentic kind of mastery. Imagine a school where every child got to experience for him- or herself genuine expertise.

Teach Oneself Something New

In 2011 I was asked to speak on a panel about what children should learn for the twenty-first century. Those of us on the panel (a teacher, a researcher, a software designer, and the directors of two schools) talked about the usual things: literacy, technology, and citizenship. At the end of the session, during the question-and-answer period, a member of the audience stood up and spoke in an elegant Indian accent. He had a self-effacing manner, and it was only later that I realized how important his own professional experience was in shaping the question he asked. He said, "In my line of work, the single most important thing is the ability to teach yourself something new. Is there a way to educate children for that?" It was a deceptively simple question. It came, as it turned out, from someone who worked at a very high level within IBM, whose headquarters were nearby. The minute I heard that, I realized I should have guessed. Nowhere is the ability to teach oneself new skills, to bootstrap oneself into expertise, and to invent as apparent as it is in the world of information technology. But IBM and Google employees are not the only ones who are better off knowing how to teach themselves something new. It is the greatest source of empowerment in the world, and frees you from all kinds of limiting circumstances. However, once children hit adolescence, many of them lose their innate capacity to teach themselves new things.

Young children come equipped with two complementary learning skills: the ability to learn on their own and the ability to learn from others. They are also born eager to do both. Just watch an infant try to master walking, or discover which toys float and which sink in a bathtub, and you'll see a determined autodidact at work. Watch a child learn to talk or figure out the intricacies of friendship, and you can see the astute anthropologist bubbling up. Paradoxically, by the time children are in school, they need to learn from others how to learn on their own.

Over the last fifty years there's been wide acceptance of an idea first put forth by Jerome Bruner in 1959. In *The Process of Education*, Bruner argued that learning how to learn was more important than what children learned.[12] In subsequent years, study after study identified the key ingredients of learning how to learn, and showed how powerful these ingredients were. Nowadays, talk of "learning how to learn" is common, and most educators readily say it's the most important educational outcome. But when you actually go into schools and look for signs that children are learning how to learn, you're likely to come up empty-handed. In reality we give kids few opportunities to figure out how to learn something. We tell them what they need to know; we often give them the information we want them to know; we tell them exactly how to learn it, whether by studying this way or that way, practicing this problem for a certain number of nights, or doing steps A, B, and C in order. Then we test them and tell them whether they've learned it or not.

But I have also witnessed inspiring examples of children explicitly learning how to teach themselves something new. In one school I visited, each child, beginning with the six-year-olds, was asked to identify something he or she wanted to learn a lot about or become good at doing. Then each child sat down with the teacher and made a loose plan for how he or she would go about learning it (including getting others to help when that was called for). This explicit focus on how we learn is a form of metacognition, long known to be a powerful boost to someone's ability to take in and retain knowledge. The children's plans were specific and concrete. Each child had to estimate how long he or she would need to become expert in his or her chosen domain. Each child had to figure out the resources needed (people, websites, places to visit, materials). At the end of several months, each child was asked whether he or she had learned enough. If so, the child gave a demonstration to the rest of the class. One child learned how to design and build small pieces of furniture, one learned how to fix old clocks, and another became the resident expert on the Silk Road. The nature of the topics didn't matter as much as the depth and flexibility of the children's expertise, which was measured not simply by a teacher but by how useful the student had become as a resource to others.

The examples I just described have another thing in common:

in learning how to teach themselves something new, these children also had a chance to experience the pleasures of learning on their own, and the pleasures of sharing their newfound expertise with others. Thus they were not simply acquiring the skills of an autodidact; they were acquiring the disposition to continue learning in any setting. A rich body of literature suggests that when adults continue to learn new things, their lives are significantly enhanced. In other words, the ability to learn new things is practical, and it helps people continue to thrive into old age.

If I Am Not for Others, What Am I?

Our schools emphasize individual achievement from the minute a child begins kindergarten. We test them individually, we ask them to work independently, and we praise their ability to keep their hands to themselves, to stay out of other people's business, and to become self-reliant. All of that would be fine if it weren't for the fact that actually we are, as Aristotle first pointed out, social animals, dependent on one another from the moment we are born until the moment we die. Self-reliance has become less and less relevant in a modern technological world, while collaboration and community have become ever more important. Getting along with people who are different from you, flourishing as a group, and taking care of others—these are at least as essential as arithmetic, spelling, or history. And they are harder to learn. For all the talk at the corporate level about teamwork (to take one strangely chilling example, see how it's ballyhooed in 2014's *The Lego Movie*) and the obvious importance in modern life of community, we put very little energy into helping children think from the perspective of others, become able to put the needs of other people ahead of our own, and learn to be adept at working in groups.

In recent years there has been a fair amount of legislation to ensure that schools insist on children being kind to one another and that bullying is addressed quickly and firmly. At the same time research has uncovered a range of techniques for helping children get along. But all too often the application of this research has been piecemeal or, worse, compartmentalized, so that a one-week program at the beginning of the school year or a set of activities introduced periodically allows the school to comply with the legislation but does little to teach children how to be thoughtful of others, collaborate, and put the needs of the group ahead of individual goals. Yet collaboration and getting along, or what some call "other-mindedness," is one of the most vital capacities children can acquire in a school setting.

In 1996 I helped start a small independent school in Bridgehampton, New York. We had hoped to make it a public school, but at the time it was not possible to establish a new charter school in New York State. Instead, we designed the school so that the cost per student matched the state average cost per student in the public school system. We were determined that the school would reflect the racial, economic, and cultural diversity of the neighborhood, which included middle-class white children and working-class black, American Indian, and Latino children (though the income of some of those families hovered right at the poverty line).

My role was to come up with an educational plan. What would children do each day, what did we hope they would learn, how would teachers teach? We were dead set on creating a strong community and encouraging children to take responsibility for one another. We felt that learning to embrace differences in others was just as important as learning to read. During those first few months, as I daydreamed about what the classrooms might look like, it came to me that the renowned Jewish scholar Hillel (born 110 BCE) offered a wonderful school philosophy: "If I am not for myself, who will be for me? If I am only for myself, what am I? If not now, when?"

How would one put such concern for others at the center of a classroom? The most interesting thing we did was to give each teacher a group of children who ranged in age from five to twelve. Our thinking was as follows: Teachers would be pushed, each and every day, to think of each child as an individual. No assumptions could be made about what a child was like or could do based on their ethnicity or their age. No lesson could be devised that was premised on a certain set of skills. Instead, any activity would have to be flexible enough so that all kinds of kids could dive into it, each at their own level. This removed teachers' safety net—a net that, in my experience, was more like a cage. Second, by mixing children of different ages, we hoped that helping one another would become a part of their daily lives.

Back at the turn of the twentieth century, the Russian psychologist Lev Vygotsky did experiments to show that not only do children learn information from other children, but their developmental trajectory is shaped by such interaction.[13] A century later, Ann Brown and others have done research showing unequivocally that when children teach one another what they have each learned, they all learn more, and learn it better. In other words, contrary to the usual practice of separating children so that they don't cheat, copy, or depend too much on one another, it seems that even from a purely cognitive perspective, learning together is good. Children who know less learn from the ones who know more, of course, but the child who knows more than her buddy also benefits cognitively by having to make her knowledge explicit. And the benefits of collaboration go beyond the academic. In order to become an adult who seeks the pleasures of community and can navigate its hazards as well, children need to work at that task as hard as they do on anything else that is both important and challenging. Isolation is one of the most destructive and debilitating conditions of life. In other words, it's not only that communities and workplaces do best when people cooperate. Humans are happiest when they can depend on others and when others can depend on them. Having friends, being members of a group (such as AA, churches, and political and other community-based organizations), and feeling enmeshed in a community are essential to well-being. The ability to live and work with others is key to a productive, happy existence. But this doesn't come as naturally as people may think. It is, to a great extent, acquired through an educational process, whether that process is formal or not. Some children learn collaboration and interdependence at home, but many do not. And the forces of modern everyday life work against selflessness, compromise, and the ability to think from other people's perspectives. If we want people, whether they are young or old, to know how to be part of a group, that learning process must become a priority in schools.

Reading

Whenever I think of children learning to read, two images pop into my head, side by side, like a split-screen television image. In one screen a little girl, head bent over her worksheet, is circling the words that rhyme. She is doing one of hundreds of similar sheets designed to teach her the components of the process of reading. If she continues to do these sheets, she is likely to be able to read a paragraph. She might even be able to tell you what is in the paragraph. If she gets a passing score on her English tests each time she's assessed, there's a good chance she'll be able to follow an instruction manual, fill out a job application, and perhaps understand a newspaper article. She'll be able to read. But that does not mean she'll be a reader. Meanwhile, on the second screen I imagine the writer Rebecca Mead as a teenager, slouched in some corner, oblivious to the sounds around her, eyes and thoughts buried in the pages of *Middlemarch*. She imagines herself as Dorothea. She wrings her hands at Dorothea's bad taste in men. Her heart soars when Dorothea bubbles over with hope and idealism. She is lost in someone else's world, thinking thoughts she'd never otherwise think.

If you walk into most elementary school classrooms, you'll see my left-hand screen again and again. The school system is designed to try to make sure that everyone can read. It does little to make sure everyone wants to read. Which is why we passively accept the idea that only a lucky handful can be like the girl on my right-hand screen. Rebecca Mead is a smart, erudite, and fortunate member of the middle class. She writes for the *New Yorker*, one of the best literary publications in the world. But should we assume that while it's essential that everyone *can* read, it's all right if only a few lucky ones actually become readers? Why not make it our educational goal for all to become readers? There is plenty of developmental research showing that all the elements of becoming a reader—a love of story, an interest in character, and the deeply human capacity to imagine alternate realities—are accessible to virtually all children.

Moreover, contrary to what the press might lead you to think, many children can read at least a simple short story or set of instructions by the time they are ten. When they cannot, the best solution often is to give them lots of one-on-one time with a skilled reader and to immerse them in a language-rich environment where books and stories are accessible, pleasurable, and meaningful. Research clearly shows that children who grow up in families where books, conversation, and stories are prevalent and where grown-ups read usually learn to read fairly easily. So these are the features that children at risk need at school. For children who are not at risk, endless worksheets about parsing sentences or correctly identifying plot devices does them little good, and plenty of harm, by keeping them from time with a good book. When people think about learning to read, they often focus on isolated academic skills: the ability to spell, to sound out words quickly and fluidly, to identify parts of a sentence, and to answer specific (and often nitpicky) questions about the text. But what they should be looking for is the child's ability and desire to become immersed in a book.

We are all better off being readers and being around others who are readers. And that is not at all the same as making sure that everyone can pass increasingly difficult or complex reading tests. Being *able* to read is only one part of the equation. You don't need to be a very fast reader, good at parsing sentences, or even good at identifying the motives of the main character to be a reader. You do need to be able to read easily enough so that you want to read more. Once you've achieved that fairly straightforward goal, the most important thing is to discover the pleasure and utility of reading, so that you will go on doing it.

A wide range of studies shows that people who read have larger vocabularies, are more effective communicators, and are more likely to construct persuasive arguments. True readers are more able to understand abstract concepts, capable of thinking about problems from several perspectives, and more likely to consider a range of information when considering whom to vote for or what policy to support. Readers, in short, are more informed citizens; it therefore follows that the more readers there are, the better off society will be. Just as important, reading enriches people's lives by allowing them to enter alternate worlds, encounter the experiences of people from distant cultures and times, and learn about things far outside their immediate realm. Research suggests that people who read novels have greater empathy and emotional insight than people who do not. In short, reading opens one's world. There is no question that all schools should still teach the mechanics of reading, but these lessons should be minimal, just enough to enable a child to break into a book. After that, our central goal should be to make every student a true reader.

I visited an elementary school on Manhattan's Upper West

Side where signs of this approach were peeking out everywhere. One in particular stood out. When I first got to the building, I noticed that all the children had the same bright, cheery book bags. It turned out that the school gave them as gifts to each child. What was in them? Every child carried with her a book she was reading and a book she hoped she could read in the future. This is deceptively simple. You might think that it's no different from assigning a child a book to read and listing a slightly harder book that you expect the child to master before the end of the year. The yellow book bags carry a different message, however. They make reading a gift and a treat. The teachers were clear that the children chose their own books. And by also asking the children to think about a book for the future, the teachers made books something to be longed for, something to aspire to. I didn't pass a single classroom in that building where at least one child wasn't curled up somewhere, reading a book from that yellow book bag. This was a school trying to ensure a society filled with readers.

Imagine that you are in charge of a school. You already have decided that in order to succeed the school will have to be a place where children want to spend their day. You realize that the first step is to articulate a compelling set of goals. These goals cannot just look good on a piece of paper in September or June, nor can they be captured in a mission statement, framed and posted on a wall, or sent out in a brochure. Instead you decide you want to come up with concrete goals that mean something specific and real in everyday life. If met, these goals will ensure that kids are leaving your school more thoughtful, more engaged, and thus happier than they otherwise would be.

A close look at schooling over the past fifty years has proven to you that it makes no sense to expect every child to be able to discuss Shakespeare or do calculus. It's not that you don't have high standards for your students. It's just that you want the *right* high standards, not the ones that you've inherited from other eras or the ones that are easiest to measure. Let's say you've also come to realize that it is a travesty to use school as a job-training program. Getting educated and getting trained for a job are different. School should be the place where children become educated.

Imagine you've thought long and hard about how schools can put children on the path to living decent, meaningful, satisfying lives. What are the abilities and dispositions that set children on that path? What would a school look like if it made happiness, rather than money, the pot of gold at the end of the rainbow? It's actually not that complicated, and it all comes down to a fairly simple list:

- Become immersed in complex and meaningful activities
- Develop a sense of purpose
- Acquire an eagerness for knowledge, and the ability to get it
- Think about things fully
- Become good at things
- Contribute to one's community
- Appreciate and understand those who are different from you
- Read for pleasure and for information

The next question is this: What would a school where children could acquire these abilities and dispositions look like?

FIVE

A Blueprint for Well-Being

Several years ago I spent the day visiting two elementary schools in lower Manhattan. When I walked into the first, I was instantly overwhelmed by the smell of bad food and dirty feet. As I made my way toward the main office, I noticed that the walls, which were painted a dull brown, had only a few tired-looking posters, which exhorted the children to try their hardest and aim for the sky. I didn't see one piece of art, nor one thing made by a child. A group of teachers passed me in the hall; they were discussing the chances of a snow day the next day, and only interrupted their conversation when one turned to tell a little boy he probably shouldn't be in the hallway. I turned a corner and came upon a row of children lining up outside their classroom, waiting to go to the cafeteria. Their teacher reminded them to keep their hands to themselves and not to dawdle or fool around. Two girls in the line began to play a little clapping game with their hands. The teacher called out sternly, "Girls, stop that. We're on line. If you cannot control yourselves, you'll each get another check, and then you'll miss ten minutes of recess. We don't have time for this. We've got to stay on schedule." I followed the group to lunch. The cafeteria was noisy and smelled stale, and the children were being told to hurry up and keep their voices down. Not one thing I saw was unusual, and each thing I saw had a perfectly reasonable justification: the school lacked money for repainting and putting art on the walls, and children have to behave when moving between classrooms or else there will be chaos. On the other hand, the atmosphere was dreary from beginning to end. Children were being rushed, chided, and constrained all of the time. Everyone seemed so focused on meeting specific objectives that any idea of school as a happy, pleasant environment in which children could flourish and enjoy themselves seemed slightly silly, a bit utopian.

Luckily, I visited another school that same day. In this school, with a similar student population and similar funding, things looked quite different. As soon as I walked through the main entrance, I was greeted by a sculpture that reminded me vaguely of work by Red Grooms. Made of papier-mâché and painted in bright colors, it was a cluster of three-foot-tall people throwing their hands up in glee. It had clearly been made by young children. As I walked down the halls, I noticed the walls were covered with stories and paintings by children. One wall had been painted like a fresco, and the title explained that it depicted the third graders' dreams. Most remarkable in that building was lunch. Each class was eating lunch in its classroom. Music was playing through speakers, and the children were sitting at small tables chatting. A grown-up was sitting at each table, also eating lunch, and joining in the conversation. It reminded me of Bryant Park in Midtown Manhattan on a summer day.

One of the worst travesties of contemporary schooling is the idea that children's day-to-day experience does not matter. They are funneled through ugly hallways, crammed into noisy cafeterias, served bad food, asked to eat in a rush, and told to think quickly. They are asked to go for hours on end with few sources of pleasure. Time spent talking to friends is considered a waste. In most of the places where children seem to thrive (such as Finland, to name a popular example), it is a given that the day should be at least somewhat enjoyable, that pleasure and work should go hand in hand. Why would we want to teach our children otherwise?

If I were to design a school where the aim was to provide children with a foundation for building a happy life, I would begin by thinking about how to create a physical and social environment that was pleasant—a place a child would like to spend the bulk of each day, where learning and trying hard would be a pleasure, not a duty. It would have to be a place that felt like it was, to some extent, *theirs*. That would mean putting their ideas and work everywhere, and creating comfortable places to sit, to socialize, and to eat. It would also mean giving children enough time so that they wouldn't always be rushing—time to make transitions between classrooms, time to get settled in, and time to eat meals. Finally, I would encourage children and their teachers to incorporate meaningful rituals into the school day. These might include starting each day with a good poem, eating good food together at lunch, and listening to music each afternoon. In her fourth-grade classroom in Chicago, Esmé Codell began each day by greeting each child at the door, shaking their hands, and giving them a chance to throw a problem into the wastebasket.[1] Then they all listened to the Pledge of Allegiance over the school loudspeaker, at the end of which they called out in unison, "Play ball!" There are many simple and perfectly delightful ways to make a group of children feel like they belong together.

Having made sure that the basic environment encouraged a sense of well-being, I'd turn to how children would spend their day. This would be a school where the emphasis was on providing children with a small number of core dispositions that equipped them not only to work but also to communicate with others, to be thoughtful, and to find or create a sense of purpose. What would such a school look like? What would be most essential, and what would become less important? What kind of day would the students have? On the following pages I propose the core elements of a school designed to promote well-being, sketching out how one would go about making a school like that work. I describe seven things children should be doing on most days of every week. But these components will work only under certain conditions, which I also outline.

Core Goals

1. Have Conversations

Think of Roosevelt and Churchill, Lerner and Loewe, or Kitty and Levin from *Anna Karenina*. What do they have in common? They talked to each other, and they listened too. In almost all times of international crisis, the best headline goes something like this: "Putin and Obama Agree to Talk." Our survival, both within and across nations, depends on our willingness to talk and our ability to do so in a genuine way. Almost all good things begin in conversation. Through conversation people exchange ideas, collaborate, resolve differences, make one another feel understood, and entertain. It is the medium that sets us apart from other species and lifts us above our baser instincts. Not only that, but conversation during the early years predicts other, seemingly unrelated but essential abilities. Children who have more conversations tend to do better in all kinds of ways as they get older. They have bigger vocabularies, do better on kindergarten tests that predict later school success, learn to read more easily, and (here's the big news) are more likely to have conversational skill when they grow up. This means they will be more able to listen to other people, more likely to use language in a way that conveys information, more able to form arguments, more able to engage in the collaborative construction of ideas, and more skilled at collective decision making. Language is not only the process that sets us apart from other species but also the key to the kind of society we currently cherish—one in which debate, exchange of ideas, collaborative problem solving, and creation of communities are at a premium. At the end of the day, the ability to listen, to speak persuasively and responsively, and to jump into a conversation with genuine interest and real information is one of the most essential skills adults can have if they are to live as thoughtful and engaged members of a community, however large or small.

There is one other important thing to keep in mind. Research has shown that children are incredibly impressionable when it comes to conversational habits. Babies and toddlers instinctively participate in conversations, and in so doing, they learn the fundamentals of discourse (how to take turns, how to ask questions, how to respond to others). But whether these basic skills blossom into a capacity for true dialogue depends on what a child hears and is invited to do during his or her next ten years. Children who engage in and hear sustained, varied, and rich conversations are much more likely to initiate and participate in such conversations themselves. Research has also shown striking differences in the language experiences of children who grow up in middle-class households and those who grow up in poverty.[2] Poor children hear far fewer words each day. Moreover, more of the words they hear are just for "business" (commands, discipline, getting through the day). Middle-class children are far more likely to hear all kinds of words, and the adults around them are far more likely to use words to describe things, tell stories, ask questions, and articulate ideas. Researchers now believe that this difference in early language environment can account for some of the most important differences between children in academic performance.

Most teachers think that lots of conversation is happening in their classrooms, because they hear so much chitchat. But actually, real conversations are given short shrift in most schools. Research has shown how few extended conversations teachers have with individual children, or even small groups of children. Nor is much attention given to the content and structure of these conversations. Moreover, children aren't given much time for sustained or far-reaching conversations with one another.

Given the findings, it's somewhat ironic that schooltime conversations are typically considered a luxury, one only the affluent or academically successful can afford, while it is assumed that children from poor backgrounds cannot dawdle around chatting when they have so much academic ground to cover. In fact, the opposite is true. The more scant a child's early language environment, the more imperative it is to provide that child with a rich language environment at school. This does *not* mean long lists of vocabulary words and more worksheets showing them how to organize a sentence. It means more opportunities to talk at length and with increasing depth, both with other children and with grown-ups, about topics that matter to them. It means more opportunities to have good conversations. Ironically, making time and opportunities for interesting conversations is much simpler and more fun than many of the activities that currently fill a schoolchild's day. And conversations have a much greater impact.

But not all conversations are alike. Conversations can be long or short, spare and to the point or wandering and multilayered. They can be one-sided or mutual. Consider the following two exchanges, each of which took place in a classroom of five-year-olds.

TEACHER: Okay, kids. What makes the four seasons happen?
FIRST CHILD: I know. I know. It's the sun.
TEACHER: Yes, but what is it about the sun?

SECOND CHILD: It's not the sun. It's the earth. The way the earth goes round in a circle. It's a—

FIRST CHILD: It is so the sun.

TEACHER: But kids, let's focus. What happens that makes the seasons? It's when the . . . ? [*The teacher waits for them to fill in the blank.*]

FIRST CHILD: It's when the earth goes around the sun.

TEACHER: Wellll, not exactly. So, what is it? Does anyone remember what we learned last week?

[*The children don't know what she's looking for, so they sit silently.*]

Now, contrast that with the following exchange, from children the same age, in another classroom in a similar community.

TEACHER: I've always wondered what would happen if one year the summer just didn't end. Whadyya think?

FIRST CHILD: What? You mean, no winter? Why?

TEACHER: I don't know. Hadn't thought that far. Why would winter not come?

SECOND CHILD: If an asteroid hit the sun.

THIRD CHILD: Then we'd all die instantly.

TEACHER: Ugh. That's not where I was going with this. I just meant, what would be different that first year?

FIRST CHILD: Hmm. Well, if there was no disaster, no asteroid, and the warm weather just went on and on and on, I guess, well, no frost? My mom's tomatoes would go on growing.

TEACHER: So far it sounds good. Anything bad?

SECOND CHILD: No colored leaves. Ew. It would get so dry. Our lawn is always brown by the end of August. Maybe it would go totally black.

THIRD CHILD: Yeah. We wouldn't die so soon. But we'd die faster.

[*The conversation continued for twenty-two more turns.*]

The first conversation is an example of what I have elsewhere called the "quiz model." The teacher uses questions to see if the children know what she wants them to know. They know that she is looking for a particular answer. It's a conversation in form only, without any real exchange of ideas or information. Neither teacher nor children show any investment or genuine interest in the topic. The children are not learning anything particularly important or useful. Just as problematic, they are losing out on a chance to practice real conversation. Instead the only likely outcome is that they'll feel good if they know the right answer to the question, or bad if they don't.

In James Thurber's classic story "The Curb in the Sky," the narrator visits his old friend Charlie Deshler, who is in a mental hospital.[3] He's been driven crazy by his intrusive wife of many years, Dottie, who interrupts him at every turn. In a desperate attempt to talk about something Dottie cannot interrupt, Charlie tells his friend, the narrator, about a dream in which he takes a trip to the moon. When he gets to the part of his dream where Santa Claus stops him, he tells his friend, "So, I pulled over to the curb." Dottie interrupts and corrects him. "No. You pulled over to a *cloud*. There aren't any curbs in the sky. There couldn't be. You pulled over to a cloud." Thurber's story is a poignant and vivid reminder that the ability to talk uninterrupted and to tell others your ideas and private thoughts without correction is essential to the human spirit.

What would it take to put conversations at the center of the classroom? One simple method is to ask children to spend more time, in small groups, talking through ideas, projects, or even just their own experiences. Consider the following two examples of literary discussions. The first was with a group of eleven- to thirteen-year-olds, the second with a group ranging in age from seven to eleven.

Twelve middle schoolers were sitting around a table, discussing the segment of *To Kill a Mockingbird* they had read the night before as homework. The teacher started the conversation:

TEACHER: Do Scout and Jem know who left the gum in the tree?

FIRST STUDENT: Not at first.

TEACHER: That's right. Who figures it out first, Jem or Scout?

SECOND STUDENT: Jem.

TEACHER: Why do you think the author tells things in such a roundabout way?

FIRST STUDENT: To keep the reader guessing?

SECOND STUDENT: It's more interesting if it's a mystery.

TEACHER: That's right.

These questions are all reasonable, all clearly intended to get the children to pay attention to details and think about why a book is written in a certain way. But the structure of the exchange leaves no room at all for a genuine exchange. Real conversations do not follow a script. Rarely does one person have all the information, while the other speakers merely offer demonstrations of their knowledge. A real conversation is somewhat wandering, includes unexpected twists and turns, and features authentic and often spontaneously constructed thoughts and opinions. Offering reactions, ideas, and impressions is not the same as supplying answers.

The following exchange is also about perspective. This one took place in a group of students ranging in age from seven to eleven, with their teacher. The teacher had been reading aloud a story called "The One and Only Ivan." The students were not gathered together to discuss the book. Instead the teacher was sitting in a chair, some kids were sitting comfortably on large beanbags, others were lying on the rug, and some were sitting at tables, quietly sketching while she read.

The teacher was reading a portion of the story in which Ivan describes his room.

CAM, AGE 7: Hey, wait a minute—is Ivan telling this whole story?

MEREDITH, AGE 11: Well, yes he is. The whole novel is told from his point of view.

CAM: But not the parts where the outside of the mall is described—he doesn't say "I see the outside of the mall."

MEREDITH: But that's how first person works—even though Ivan doesn't say "I see the outside of the mall," you already know it's from his point of view and you don't need his eyes for everything. And sometimes the readers need to see things the character can't see.

[CAM shrugs.]

TEACHER: All excellent points—so you don't need the "I" or his eyes in every statement in the book in order for it to be told from Ivan's point of view. It is interesting to think about the differences between first person and third person. Does anyone want to talk about those differences?

MIRA, AGE 9: Well, third person is when there isn't one person in the story telling it—there is a narrator that you don't really know.

ADRIAN, AGE 8: Oh, like all the Dr. Seuss books—they're all told in third person. I thought when we were talking about Ivan, you [he points to Meredith] were saying that all books are told in the first person and I was thinking, "No way, not Dr. Seuss!" [Looking happily relieved] I get it now.

[CAM asks the teacher to continue reading.]

Sometimes teachers can guide such conversations with a little input, so that children who aren't particularly adept at the implicit rules of conversation can learn them. One teacher I observed years ago had a talking stick. Whoever held it had the floor, and everyone else was supposed to focus on that person. He or she then got to choose whom to hand the talking stick to next. When I first saw this in action, shortly after the children had been introduced to the concept, I felt the rules were stifling. Watching the children, it seemed to me that they couldn't get any flow going, or any sense of immersion in the topic itself, because they were so focused on passing the stick. But when I returned only one month later, I saw that the children barely noticed the stick as it moved around the circle, and that having this one simple and very visceral rule allowed them to really listen to one another and contribute to a genuine exchange of ideas. Though it took some getting used to, the payoff was huge, and along the way the children learned how much value their teacher placed on genuine discussion.

Children also need to be allowed to talk about things that matter to them. It is almost impossible to have a good conversation when you don't care much about the topic (the importance of agriculture to Western civilization, what the literary technique of foreshadowing is, or how electricity works). In other words, all too often children are invited to speak on topics about which they have no sense of commitment or urgency. Luckily, there is no shortage of topics that grab them. In a wonderful demonstration of an alternative approach, Catherine Snow and her colleagues asked middle school students in Boston public schools to plan debates on topics in which they had a great interest. During the weeks when the children were planning and then conducting their debates, their vocabulary, sentence structure, and powers of argument were exponentially greater.[4]

Conversation is one of the most powerful tools to be acquired in school. To the uninitiated, it may seem ephemeral, loose, unpredictable, and hard to manage. But just because it can appear informal, sprawling, and fun shouldn't confuse teachers, parents, or educational administrators into thinking it's unimportant. It's one of the most valuable intellectual tools a child can acquire. Any visitor to a classroom should be impressed, not dismayed, to see children talking to one another and to grown-ups.

2. Read

I often ask people to tell me about a book that has changed them in some specific and concrete way. Sometimes people can quickly and easily think of a title. A middle-aged woman once said to me, "I read *Wuthering Heights* when I was twelve. It was the first time I realized that there was a way to describe what I yearned for day after day. It suddenly wasn't my dark secret. It was something powerful, something other people felt too!" A young man told me, "When I was fourteen my aunt gave me a copy of E.O. Wilson's autobiography. After that I took all the biology courses I could. I knew I loved the outdoors. But Wilson's book showed me there was a world beneath that world, which I wanted to know about, just like he did." A woman in her thirties from Vermont said, "*Little Women*. It changed me before there was a me to change. Jo March gave my mother a run for her money in the women-I-could-grow-up-to-be category. It was the first character I got angry with, because I felt she was better than some of the decisions she was making. I think it was my first understanding of adulthood that wasn't synonymous with parenthood or authority." One man said, "It was last week. I read a new book called *We Are All Completely Beside Ourselves*. I will never look at the animal world in the same way." Others have offered more down-to-earth examples. Said one woman, "After I read *Julie and Julia* I decided I was going to learn to cook." Another said, "It's not the books. It's the writer. No one understands me like Stephen King. He's as close a companion as anyone I actually know." But not everyone has answers like this. In fact, the vast majority of people I've asked have no clue what I'm even talking about. They think one reads to take one's mind off the day or to get practical information. The idea that books would be a central part of your life, shaping the way you think, feel, and act, is completely strange to them.

The writer Joyce Carol Oates recently listed just a handful of notable books in which people have recounted powerful relationships with a single book or an author:

Nicholson Baker's quirkily inspired book-length essay, *U and I*, charts his youthful obsession with the sensuous, poised prose and public career of John Updike, yielding a curious double portrait that manages to be both self-effacing and arrogant. Geoff Dyer's *Out of Sheer Rage: Wrestling with D.H. Lawrence* is a very funny if despairing account of the writer's failure to produce the "sober, academic study" of Lawrence's work he has hoped to achieve, before becoming overcome by distractions and inertia and creating a "wild book" in its place. Christopher Beha's *The Whole Five Feet: What the Great Books Taught Me About Life, Death, and Pretty Much Everything Else* is a warmly personal account of a young man's intensive reading of the Harvard Classics (51 volumes) amid a season of familial crisis and loss. Phyllis Rose's ironically titled *The Year of Reading Proust: A Memoir in Real Time* subordinates the magisterial *Remembrance of Things Past* to the busy, often trivial minutiae of the memoirist's daily life, while, as its ebullient title suggests, David Denby's *Great Books: My Adventures with Homer, Rousseau, Woolf and Other Indestructible Writers of the Western World* is a zestful anecdotal account of an adult returning to the education he'd failed to appreciate as a Columbia undergraduate. And there is Rick Gekoski's chatty *Outside of a Dog: A Bibliomemoir*, which traces the influence of 25 books on the English bookseller-author's life.[5]

These writers magnify what is sometimes true, albeit in a more casual and perhaps more private way, for ordinary, everyday readers: books aren't something you go to just for a piece of information or a moment of entertainment. At best, they can permeate your psychological life and deeply affect your thoughts, your aspirations, and your understanding of the world. But readers can be strongly influenced at a more prosaic level by what they read as well. The mystery writer Laura Lippman describes it this way:

> My reading life is like an airport where a bunch of planes circle in a holding pattern, then—boom, boom, boom, several come in for a landing. So I have three: Helen FitzGerald's *The Cry*, Elizabeth Hand's *Illyria*, and Tom Nissley's *A Reader's Book of Days*. *The Cry* tackles the toughest subject in crime fiction, the death of an infant, and it surprised me, which is rare when I'm reading crime fiction. Hand's book is a Y.A. literary mashup of *Flowers in the Attic* and Noel Streatfeild's *Theater Shoes*. Nissley's book offers monthly reading lists, and I'm a sucker for such lists. January includes H.P. Lovecraft, Zadie Smith and Arthur Hailey—what's not to love?[6]

Why should such intense and serious reading be only for the privileged? Anyone can be a reader, though if you do not grow up in a family of readers, school is the best way to become one. Zoe, an eleven-year-old girl whose schoolwork I was reviewing, wrote, "I used to only read short fiction books with pictures on every page before I started going to school. Now I read thick heavy memories [i.e., memoirs] with no pictures whatsoever! Ask anyone. You almost never see me without a book. I love reading, and it's all because of school."

Although it may not always be the case, for now reading is still the essential activity that usually transforms people's intellectual lives. Through reading, people can learn about things they have never, or will never, encounter—faraway places, people who live in other countries, things that happened long ago, perspectives foreign to their experience, and unlikely or impossible events. Reading requires and elicits complex thought, and often leads to a level of deliberation and analysis that is too easily bypassed in the hustle and bustle of everyday life. As Catherine Snow, among others, has shown, when children become readers they are more likely to take the perspective of others, evaluate evidence, and analyze other people's reasons and facts in a closer way. At the highest levels (say, those who go to good colleges or undertake study at the graduate level) these skills can be practiced and honed with great rigor. But for most people, a modicum of these skills can easily be attained just by reading a lot.

However, there is quite a difference between knowing how to read and being a reader. Instead of pushing all children—quite futilely, it turns out—to analyze perspective, discuss literary techniques, and show that they can answer endless questions about the structure of a story, we should spend more time and energy helping children take pleasure in reading. It's been done, here and there, with great success.

In her book *Educating Esmé*, Esmé Codell writes vividly about making the book corner the most inviting place in the room.[7] Children need time to read, and they need to be able to listen to stories read aloud, without a quiz or assignment looming over them. Who would want to read if you knew that at the end of each chapter or book you'd have to answer a series of questions? Of course, schools must figure out how to make sure that children who can't read aren't slipping through the cracks. Teachers must beware of the child sitting with a book in front of his face who is going through the gestures but not really reading. There are all kinds of simple techniques for helping individual children overcome specific obstacles to reading. But many children who seem to have difficulty would struggle less if they were immersed more thoroughly in conversations, heard more books read aloud, and had more time to read things they liked. Reading lessons and spending hours a day in a reading culture are different things. If schools became infused with reading culture, there would still be kids who couldn't crack the code, and they would still need more targeted help. But if we focus on cultivating readers rather than honing a set of reading skills, far fewer children will struggle with the important aspects of reading.

3. Lean on One Another

Most parents, teachers, and policy makers agree that getting along with others, knowing how to be part of a group, and collaborating are essential to civilized life. And yet most schools leave this to chance. Why not make collaboration a central focus of a child's daily experience at school? There are some straightforward ways to do this.

Just after the 1954 *Brown v. Board of Education* Supreme Court decision to desegregate schools, plenty of classrooms were thrown into disarray. Paradoxically, many children of color who were sent to predominantly white schools suffered even greater academic and personal problems than they'd had when they attended segregated and often inferior schools, for in the newly integrated schools racial tensions often only increased.

In communities near the Mexican border, Latino children sent to integrated schools felt even worse about not speaking English like the other kids, and the apparent differences between the children in academic performance seemed to grow wider. In Austin, Texas, the school superintendent invited in a group of social psychologists to observe what was happening and help find a solution. After weeks of observation, the group ended up seeing something paradoxical: by being pushed into the same space, each group's self-concept and attitudes toward the other groups merely hardened. Being together, in and of itself, did not reduce stereotypes or nudge kids into figuring out how to get along. So the psychologists devised a very specific and somewhat sneaky plan for manipulating the kids into changing their attitudes and working together. They put the children into what they called jigsaw arrangements.[8] White children and Latino or black children would work together preparing for a test or the completion of an academic unit. Each child in the group would be responsible for a particular section of information (if they were learning about the English Reformation, for example, one would study Queen Elizabeth, one would study the influence of the Pope, one would study Thomas Cromwell, and so on). Each child knew something all the other children in the group needed to know in order to do well. This arrangement forced the children to be dependent on one another.

The psychologists devised this scheme by drawing on the theory of cognitive dissonance. The theory predicts that when a person holds two opposing thoughts, he or she experiences discomfort, and in an effort to reduce that discomfort the person is forced to change one of the thoughts or come up with a new justification for the two thoughts. The psychologists speculated that it would be hard for a white child to have a low opinion of a black or Latino child on whom he or she depended for success. The white child would feel uncomfortable needing help from someone he or she thought poorly of, so in order to resolve that dissonance, the psychologists predicted, the white child would revise his or her view of the nonwhite child. In turn, black and Latino children in these groups would begin to feel better about their participation and their relationships within the classroom. Sure enough, their academic performance improved, and so did their self-esteem. Within months racial tensions had been dramatically reduced. This is an example of a very deliberate effort to help kids who are different get along.

When my college students read about the jigsaw classroom, they often object, "I had to do group projects when I was a kid. It drove me crazy that my grade was dependent on some other kid who wasn't as smart, or maybe was just lazy, or didn't care as much about school." It's true that working together can be frustrating: things don't always play out fairly, and being part of a group can sometimes hold one back. But these difficulties only make it more imperative that we help children learn how to manage it, because the rewards of collaboration are even more tremendous than the perils.

In 2007 a small group of high school students in western Massachusetts started a garden with the intention of providing their school cafeteria with local organic food. Within nine months, more than two hundred students in the school district, ranging in age from five to eighteen, had helped out on a regular basis. The thing worth noting about a garden is that collaboration is not an add-on idea. In order to grow enough vegetables to feed two thousand children, people have to work together. In a project such as a garden, no one has to invent a way to make people interdependent. The only thing that requires some thought and creativity is figuring out how to teach children better ways of working together so that they don't learn all the same bad habits displayed by most adults. One of the things the students came up with was a sign-up sheet so that everybody didn't all show up to water the beds on the same morning. They became good at delegating tasks, so that some weeded, some planted, some ordered seeds, some devised new watering systems, and some harvested. They were forced to choose work that fit the capabilities of students of different ages: the kindergarteners did less planting and more harvesting, while the juniors and seniors applied for grants and put up a greenhouse. Last but not least, they made time to celebrate their successes. The group had feasts on the edge of the garden, stopped work to gather and eat their first watermelons, and organized a community pig roast in the spring. They learned quickly that having fun and accomplishing things together went hand in hand, and that what they could learn as individuals was much greater when they worked as a group. Their goal was not to learn specific content or skills, as is usually the case in school, nor was the goal learning to work together. Rather, the goal was to grow a garden.

Too often teachers think about what activity or lesson they want children to master (multiplication problems, the U.S. Constitution, or understanding how electricity works) and then put students in groups, hoping that group work will make the lesson more appealing or that they can efficiently incorporate some "team building" while sticking to the curriculum. Under these circumstances, children are likely to skate right past the collaboration itself, instead focusing on what they need to learn. They will tolerate the group or they may even enjoy it. But they won't learn anything new about communal life.

We know that people learn best when they are learning things that matter to them. It's not enough to periodically add a group activity that has little other significance to the children or the curriculum. If we want children to learn how to work together, we have to give them work they care about that requires team effort. Moreover, we have to give them time and guidance to do this in a way that goes beyond their and our instincts—the instinct of aggression, of tuning people out, or of putting one's own needs ahead of the group's.

The ability to embrace others who are not like you, to work together toward a goal, and to support the good of the group over self-interest—these capacities are so important, and so difficult, that they deserve to be moved from the periphery and be made into a central part of the school day.

4. Investigate

Children are born investigators. But in school they can learn to build on this potent and vital inclination. A child who wants to find things out, and knows how to do so, holds the keys to the universe. Investigation is not simply a set of research methods children learn a few times a week in science class. It is a way of life—a disposition to gather information in all kinds of situations.

Investigation can be built into the fabric of classroom life. Helping children become habitual investigators begins by offering them a chance to find answers to their real questions, not the ones they're told to ask. This requires a simple but often elusive shift in teaching practice. Teachers need to spend significant time on a regular basis figuring out what their students want to know and then giving students time and guidance in seeking answers. Sometimes the questions students ask require conducting actual experiments. Just as often, however, their questions can be answered by asking others, observing people and the natural world, looking things up online, and trying things out. When children are very young, it's hard to prevent them from poking, asking, tinkering, and exploring. What schools need to do is to build on this natural inclination rather than to stifle it. Students need time and resources with which to investigate. Finally, children need a chance to assess whether they have answered their own questions. How many times have we heard students (whether they are seven years old or twenty years old) say, "Is this what you wanted us to do?" They have learned how to focus on meeting someone else's requirements, but not how to figure out whether they've answered their own questions. Yet one of the key components of good scientific inquiry is figuring out whether your data answer the question you originally asked. Scientists often realize they haven't found out what they wanted to, and so they decide to keep investigating. Other times they get the answer they were looking for, which leads them to refine new questions. In order to develop the habit of inquiry, one must practice from an early age.

Ironically, research has shown that satisfying one's curiosity is one of life's greatest satisfactions. And as is the case with many appetites, satiation lasts for only a while. The child who has been encouraged to feel curious and taught how to explore and answer questions is likely to go on doing so, and be the richer for it.

5. Be Useful

Up until the nineteenth century, children were both a burden and a help to their families. In many cases they were so helpful they were unduly exploited. By the time factories replaced farms and small workshops, children weren't just helping out at home. They had become part of the workforce. The depictions in Dickens's works provide a fairly good picture of the lives of many children in the middle of the nineteenth century. But as child labor laws took effect, a different way of thinking about children seeped into Western consciousness. We began to see children as fundamentally different from adults. Psychologists began to describe unique features of the child mind. Research showed that children not only knew less than adults but also thought differently. Educators and researchers began to emphasize the value of play, freedom, and benevolent tolerance toward children. We understood that it would take children many years to become adult-like, and that during those years they would benefit from activities specially suited to their childish needs.

Many of the changes made in our educational practices in order to meet the needs of children have been wonderful. Most schools no longer allow corporal punishment. Some schools provide young children with plenty of adult supervision, interesting play materials, objects that enable hands-on learning, and lessons that at least in some ways seem attuned to the tastes and rhythms of young children. But all of our supposed knowledge about how to help children learn in school has had one very unfortunate side effect: we have made children useless. For most children, school is an exercise in long-postponed gratification, the lure being that someday they will be successful. If they are lucky enough to be in a nice school, they will have the satisfaction of time with friends, some fun things to do, and perhaps even the thrill of a good grade, an award, or a skill they didn't have before, but the work itself will not affect anyone else. Yet even children need to feel that what they do matters to others. If we want children to learn the satisfaction of making things that are beautiful and useful to others, why not let them begin when they are young?

When children do work that will be used or appreciated by others, trying to do a good job comes naturally. Writing a better story in order to improve one's grade is not nearly as natural as writing a better story so that others will be entertained or to change another person's mind. Educators worry endlessly about the rubrics used to evaluate children's work. The rubrics are designed simply to evaluate how much a child has mastered, or to compare one child to another. But what if instead children (and their teachers) evaluated what they had made or done by judging whether it was useful, interesting, informative, or beautiful to other people?

When I suggested to a group of teachers that they organize what their students did in terms of endeavors, rather than topics or themes, my thinking was that if children made things for other people to use, they would approach their work with a greater level of interest, commitment, energy, and desire for excellence. One teacher who was studying geography with her students had the class discuss the different kinds of maps people use: maps that allow you to get from one place to another quickly, maps that identify particular kinds of locations, maps that provide important historical information, and maps that tell some more idiosyncratic or personal story. Groups of children set out to design various new maps of the region where they all lived. When spring came they did not submit their work to the teacher to be graded or to get her comments. Instead, they sent their maps out to people in the community, asking them to use the maps to find specific locations and objects. The students followed up to find out how well their maps had worked. It was quickly apparent who had succeeded in mapmaking and who had not.

Children can learn that intellectual achievement affects everyone, and that the skills and knowledge they acquire can be used to improve not just their own lives but also the lives of others. By giving children things to do that are useful, children experience the pleasures of contributing to the community around them in an authentic way. And with some good guidance, they learn how to strive for excellence in such work.

6. Get Immersed, Become an Expert

Wander into any playground and you will see children, whether they are five or eleven, sweating, red-faced, and focused, intent upon whatever they are doing: swinging on swings, playing ball, making a fort, or selecting teams for capture the flag. Children know how to concentrate, and they gravitate toward complete immersion. That zest for industry is one of the most valuable characteristics of youth. Oddly, school tends to squelch it rather than build on it. It is true that when children are little, they find it hard to harness their capacity for engagement and direct it toward pursuits that are not instantly engaging. Learning to engage in activities that aren't always or quickly captivating is a valuable outcome of the educational process. But most of the time our schools don't even try to help children become engaged. They are satisfied instead with obedience and duty. The result of this is that children may lose any chance of becoming absorbed in everyday activities. When I asked a well-known superintendent of a major city school system whether the students in his schools were out of control, the veins in his neck bulged out. "Oh my God, no. The opposite. They're so well behaved it seems like they're on Demerol. But do they care about anything they're doing? Absolutely not."

At school, every child should be doing at least one thing that he or she finds really absorbing on a regular basis. Once the child has identified what that thing is, he or she needs the opportunity to develop that absorption to its fullest capacity. But the schedule in most schools works against such a sustained, effortful involvement. Forty-five-minute periods, frequent transitions, and external a priori ideas about what constitutes "excellent" and "finished" all get in the way of children's tendency to dive into something with their full energy and capacity.

Years ago I was an onlooker as a group of middle school children embarked on their annual project fair, similar to science fairs held in schools throughout the country. In this particular suburban school, the fair was for arts and sciences, which meant that a child could pick almost any topic for a project. One child, whose father was handy, chose to make a blue birdhouse out of a kit. Another did a series of posters about sports. A third wrote a book of poems. The projects gave the students a chance to do something more hands-on, more imaginative, and more individualized than the regular curriculum. On the final day the children all brought their projects into the gym, where they were set up on tables with small posters explaining how the projects were done. A team of teachers walked from project to project, rating them using a pre-established rubric. At the end of the day, the students took their projects home, and that was that.

Projects like this are nice, and they break up the academic routine. But they rarely provide students with any serious experience of immersion or intensity. In fact, in many schools students who want to "do well" focus so much on managing their assignments, meeting the criteria of the rubrics, and handing their work in on time that they consciously choose manageable projects rather than ones they have a deep affinity for, cannot resist, or long to be better at. And students who avoid challenge or don't care so much about their grades just flip the whole thing off.

Yet I have seen it work differently. In some schools, teachers make it a top priority to help their students identify something they really love, are good at, or want to be good at, and then give them time to pursue it. These endeavors cannot possibly all be symmetrical. Some children want to spend hours and hours writing comic books, others want to learn to play an instrument, and still others cannot get enough information about wars. Rather than tone these interests down or try to make them fit into one particular mold, teachers should see encouraging them as a top priority. Midway through the year, a teacher should be able to list a central interest of each child, and identify times during each week that the child is pursuing that interest. Involvement and increasing the level of mastery, depth, or range should be the goal, not a particular set of accomplishments. All those years ago when I watched the middle schoolers doing their art and science projects, one boy chose to make clay tiles illustrating scenes from *The Odyssey*. He read Robert Fagles's translation, made his own clay using ancient techniques (explained in YouTube lessons), and hung from each tile the specific sections of the text he had chosen and copied onto rolled paper scrolls. He then mounted them on a wall in his school. He spent weeks and weeks doing little else. His teachers chastised him for letting other things slide. He was told it had taken too much time and that his tiles were too drab (he used the same kind of slip, or glaze, that was used in ancient times). Clearly, immersion was not part of the rubric his teachers were using.

7. Know and Be Known by an Adult

My grandmother Henrietta grew up on the Lower East Side of Manhattan. Like many children of Eastern European Jewish immigrants, Henrietta was very poor as a child, but also intent upon doing well at school. Like many other poor children in New York City at that time, she took a secretarial course in high school rather than following a more academic program. But she remembered her school days vividly. What she remembered best, even seventy years later, was that her third-grade teacher had given her a gift of a storybook, which she treasured well into adulthood. The teacher had also given my grandmother a doll. Imagine a teacher giving a student a small gift, not intended for academic improvement, but just as a sign of affection. Imagine the impact such a gift might have on a child who otherwise could easily feel like a cog in a large machine.

One of the most powerful things schools provide children is a chance to know and be known by an adult outside of their immediate family circle. Whether one's family is attentive, high-functioning, loving, struggling, fractured, or distant, part of the essential task of childhood is to gradually build outside relationships, not only with peers but also with elders. Anyone who has even one good memory of school recalls the particular teacher who meant something to him or her. Too often we focus on the amazing, inspired teacher who made a difference because he or she was just so fabulous. But not all teachers can be fabulous, nor need they be. It *is* essential, however, that each child spend time in the unhurried company of a teacher who genuinely likes and knows that child. Though some schools have attempted to do this by assigning children to small groups who begin the day with a teacher or advisor, these relationships and the settings in which they are supposed to unfold are usually pretty perfunctory and therefore useless. The chances of a child forming an authentic relationship go way up when the adult actually does something meaningful and sustained with that student (teaching them math, coaching them in soccer, building a garden, cooking meals, or helping them choose books). The intellectual and emotional value of these relationships is so important, it is worth the time and energy it takes to ensure that they happen.

In one school I know, the teachers meet every Friday afternoon beginning at one o'clock to plan, discuss curriculum, and develop new projects. But each and every week, they also go through the complete list of student names. After each name is mentioned, someone in the room must be able to say that he or she has had a prolonged and meaningful exchange with that student, and someone must be able to say something specific about what the student has been working on and how he or she is. Usually it's the child's classroom teacher, but not always. Sometimes it's the facilities manager, the art teacher, a coach, or the person who oversees lunch preparation and service.

If a school focused with unflagging attention on the tasks of making sure that each child has prolonged and meaningful conversations with adults and other children, has many opportunities to read things that are useful and/or interesting, is nudged day in and day out to gather and examine various kinds of evidence, has on a regular basis dived into something deeply and tried to develop expertise at it, has a lively and reciprocal relationship with an adult, and has become part of a community, it would be doing a pretty good job for all of its students. These students, even if they lacked various kinds of specific skills, would be in a strong position to attain such skills as needed. They would be poised for a meaningful and satisfying life.

Conditions for Meeting These Goals

Zeroing in on these central goals would change the daily lives of teachers, transform children's educational experiences, and lead to very different outcomes. But it's not enough to identify these goals and imagine the activities that might lead to them. Schools must create the conditions where such goals are likely to be met. What are those conditions?

Community

When the educator Dennis Littky created four public high schools in Providence, Rhode Island, in 1993, he gave each school a name: Justice, Unity, Equality, and Liberty. Each student in those schools had a small buddy group and a teacher who worked with him or her for most of the day. The group started and ended each day in a meeting. During the day the teacher spent significant time with individual students, but also with pairs of students. There was plenty of time in the day for casual conversation, the kind had by people who like and know one another. After the day was over, the teacher followed up with students by phone as needed. The teachers also spent significant time talking to one another and bringing their groups together for discussions and celebrations. By putting so much emphasis on cultivating personal relationships, the school was transformed from a building containing students and teachers doing disparate tasks into an actual community.

Some schools encourage a similar sense with school slogans, uniforms, and traditions that make people feel they are part of a group. But even more important are the daily practices of group members. People feel like they are a part of a community when they help one another, work toward a common cause, share rituals, and make decisions together. In order to create a genuine sense of community, one that is more than skin deep, school leaders will often have to put other priorities aside. Students may have to have fewer class meetings or do less homework in order to have time to grow gardens, help others in the neighborhood, meet to make decisions about school governance, and celebrate one another's accomplishments. If these activities are perfunctory and dull, they won't work. Most people know the difference between real community and sham community. Schools have to be the real thing.

Reasonable Amounts of Time

One of the most important ways to help children be happy in school and acquire habits that will increase their well-being in adult life is to give them time—time to work, talk, make transitions, and explore their intellectual and physical environments without rushing. Teachers too need to slow down so that the whole day isn't a frantic shuffle from one demand to another.

Simplicity

In order to optimize the chances that the goals listed earlier will be reached by most students, it is absolutely essential that teachers and students have much shorter checklists: fewer but more important skills to be tracked, fewer but richer and more interesting topics to explore, and fewer tasks to juggle. Children should have a few things to be working on, and plenty of help and time for doing so. Teachers should have fewer goals to achieve, and more opportunity to do everything they can to achieve those goals. Ted Sizer said this in his 1992 book about high schools, *Horace's Compromise*, when he argued that in high schools "less is more."[9] But in the ensuing two and a half decades the opposite has happened. Most schools seem like they are operating on the basis of the motto "more is more." Teachers have longer and longer lists of things for which they are responsible, making it less and less likely that any meaningful items on the list will be accomplished in any real way. I'll give one example to illustrate how this plays out.

Several years ago Massachusetts passed a law requiring public schools to devise a plan for reducing bullying and for encouraging what was being referred to at the time as a "good school climate." I was asked to serve on the committee tasked with developing such a plan for my local district. As I sat there with administrators, parents, teachers, and adjustment counselors, listing the team-building activities, conflict resolution kits, evaluation forms, systems for writing up students who bullied, and curricula designed to encourage prosocial behavior and to warn against the evils of hurting others, I saw the teachers' shoulders sag lower and lower. Finally one of them tentatively raised his hand and spoke. "I really believe in all this. I think it's so important that we help these kids get along," he said. "But honestly, these meetings are getting me down. I've just added six more items to the list of things I rush to get through each week. There isn't one second in the day when I'm not hustling myself and my kids to finish some task that someone has told us is critical. I'm not sure how much more I can fit in the day." Such crowding may work in a factory (though it may not work there either), but it certainly doesn't make for a good environment for children. There is nothing educationally valuable about hustling all day long.

Autonomy

Study after study, with both children and adults, shows that having some autonomy and choice is key to a sense of well-being. For students to thrive in school, learn how to make choices, and be able to handle independence in adulthood, they must have opportunities to do so in academic settings as well as in their home lives. In other words, having some freedom to figure out what to do, how long to do it, and whom to do it with helps children be happier and like school. It leads to greater zest and involvement with what they are doing, and it also helps them acquire the ability to exercise such autonomy as they get older.

Often children's autonomy at school is so circumscribed as to be meaningless: they can choose writing prompt #1 or #2, they can build a diorama or make a collage, they can play soccer or volleyball. But these are not genuine choices, and children know it. How to spend their time, what questions merit the hard work of finding answers, and whether a piece of work requires revision are the kinds of decisions children should learn how to make while in school. Such decision making takes time, adult guidance, and support. In some schools, students are asked to decide what kind of expertise they seek, and then helped to figure out what they'd need to do to develop such expertise. They're also given a chance to make false starts, or even work hard on something that fails. In those cases, teachers see their role as facilitating the child's developing autonomy rather than making sure the child learns some specified skill or body of knowledge.

As for teachers, they too need autonomy. If they are smart enough and committed enough to be teachers, they should be trusted (and expected) to make decisions about what kinds of activities their students should work on, how to organize their students' daily schedule, and when to put one goal aside in order to work hard on another goal. They should have the freedom to choose books their students will like (and that they like) and to use methods that seem best suited to the children in their particular classroom. Good supervision should not involve telling them what to do, but instead should help them do better what they want to do.

Teachers Who Like What They Do

This "condition" is so important I have saved it for last. Research on family life has shown that children thrive when their parents feel some level of safety and happiness. Children suffer when their parents suffer. Stress, depression, illness, poverty, instability, and uncertainty all have a dramatic impact on children's intellectual, physical, and emotional development and well-being. Strangely, this essential lesson from studies of family life has not been used to think about schools. If happy parents are so essential to children's well-being, why wouldn't the same be true of the adults with whom children spend their weekdays? There is every reason to believe that children will learn more effectively, will enjoy their days at school more fully, and will develop into healthier and stronger adults when they spend their days with teachers who feel some sense of security, pleasure in what they do, and autonomy. Creating good conditions for teachers is not only good for the teachers but good for the students.

In recent years policy makers, philanthropists, and many parents have been hell-bent on weeding out bad teachers, implementing penalties for ineffective teaching, and coming up with more objective and rigorous ways to measure teacher performance. The underlying assumption is that if we got rid of bad teachers, we'd have good schools, though there is absolutely no logic to that. Moreover, this zeal for hunting down weak teachers has neglected a number of central facts of human nature. Just as most people want to do well at their work and few try to be bad at their job, most teachers want to do well and few set out to be bad. Unfortunately, having your superiors watch your every move and look for ways to rate you or catch you slipping is not the way to help struggling or weak teachers improve, and it's likely to harm the performance of good teachers. In fact, many of the regulations and constraints imposed on schools in recent years have made teaching distasteful to the most passionate, skilled, and talented educators. Most of the recent changes intended to raise the level of teaching have simultaneously weakened struggling teachers and repelled good teachers. Why not try the opposite approach? Why not put a lot of energy into helping struggling teachers do better and good teachers excel?

There are some concrete ways to make this work. Teachers need time to talk every week about their teaching: not the curriculum, not test scores, not even particular children, just the craft of teaching. In one school where I worked we got a local grocery store to donate sandwiches and cookies for a monthly lunch meeting on the craft of teaching. The only rule of these lunchtime discussions was that teachers couldn't talk about government, the union, bad parents, or bad kids. At each lunch one teacher began by talking about something that had gone wonderfully well or had failed miserably. The teachers found this slightly awkward at first, as it was so different from their weekly team meetings or faculty meetings. They needed a little nudging to keep from trying to impress one another or hide their greatest vulnerabilities. But slowly it began to catch on. Teachers started saying things like "It's so amazing to have a chance just to think and talk together. I forgot how much I loved thinking about kids and how they act." One day the teacher who had started off the meeting came up to me in the hall. A twenty-year veteran who was known in the school as a standout social studies teacher, he was knowledgeable, kind, skillful with young teens, and deeply engaged with his subject matter. But he was also very quiet—in fact, he had never spoken in a faculty meeting, and never volunteered to join in any group work with his colleagues. "I wasn't happy with what I said in there," he told me. "I didn't really get to the idea I had meant to. But I haven't been able to stop thinking about it. May I write about it?" I was startled, as clearly he had never been invited before to think out loud with colleagues about his own teaching practice. And, strangely, he felt timid, as if he needed permission to pursue the topic in writing. Six weeks later he handed me a forty-page essay on how he practices his craft. It was one of the most lucid, specific, and inspiring pieces I'd read about teaching in many years. He said he found himself just writing and writing. He hadn't realized how much he knew and wanted to say. All it took were some sandwiches, a lunch period, and an invitation to think with others about his craft.

In another school I visited, teachers take turns writing articles about education for a school publication that comes out twice a year and is disseminated to the larger community of parents, alums, and educators from neighboring schools. Though it's a lot of work for the authors contributing to any given issue, it also gives everyone a chance periodically to reflect on what they do, to share their knowledge with others, and to celebrate their own accomplishments as teachers.

There are other ways to create such a sense of interest, community, and support among teachers. One year the school where I was working secured a relatively small grant to support a summer fellowship involving six meetings in June, July, and August. We chose two books for all the fellows to read, and then divided the fellows into groups and asked each group to choose one book for their group. In other words, all we did was create book clubs (we didn't even specify what kind of book; it could be a novel, essays, a book on education, or a scientific report, as long as they felt it would spark discussion). At the end of the summer each group was asked to create a presentation—visual or verbal, informal or formal—to convey to the others what they had learned, thought, or argued about over the summer. I have rarely seen a group of teachers so excited and fired up. Many spontaneously said that it was the first time in their teaching careers that they had been paid to think. Imagine a teacher not feeling that way most of the time. How could that be good for children?

The point here is really quite simple. For students to thrive in school and develop habits that lead to well-being, they need to be around adults who like what they do and feel good about it. Schools must spend time and resources creating environments that support good teaching rather than focusing on bad teaching. Psychological research has shown, for almost a hundred years now, that people do much better when they are rewarded for good behavior than when they are punished for bad behavior. We know that's true for children. It's just as true for adults.

A young man I know, just out of college, was trying to climb the ladder in the world of banking and finance. His firm had a policy of firing the bottom 20 percent of its staff every three months. So every three months my young friend hid in the bathroom, under a friend's desk, or behind the door in the coffee room, just hoping not to be fired that month. That may work when the only outcome you are looking for is more dollars. It's not a recipe for success if you want a group of happy, thriving children who are learning from the adults around them. Schools where children thrive must be schools where good teachers—not superstars, just good ones—thrive.

The key idea here is not whether there are seven or five or eight components. Nor is it important whether everyone agrees exactly with the way I've characterized these components. What matters is the idea that in order to provide the greatest number of children with a good education in the truest sense of that word, it is essential to identify the few practices that are most likely to lead to important dispositions, and think about how to teach those well. Long laundry lists of skills, information, and activities that keep students, teachers, and administrators rushing around checking things off do not make for good learning environments, and they don't yield good outcomes. When teachers and administrators zero in on a few things and try to do them well, everyone is better off. I sometimes find it helpful to imagine what it would be like if a group of children (any group of children, from any background) finished high school genuinely loving to read, able and eager to work with others different from themselves, capable of thinking about an idea thoroughly, knowing how to become good at something, and hoping to learn more. If teachers could focus on those few things, they'd have a much higher success rate, to much greater effect.

SIX

What We Should Measure

We are a nation that measures what we love, and loves what we measure. We weigh ourselves, keep track of our cholesterol counts, and, increasingly, measure the value of a movie or a book in terms of the number of copies sold. We are dizzy with the potential of our modern tools of measurement and the power they appear to offer us.

There are many cases in which such precision has been a boon. For instance, in medicine, new tests have allowed us to identify women who might be at the greatest risk for the most dangerous forms of breast cancer. We can identify babies for whom dairy products would be deadly. We are able to predict storms and better prepare for them. But, as some scientists have argued, these tests can also be overused or used in the wrong way. The physician Ezekiel Emanuel has argued that many of the medical tests people rush to take, year in and year out, cost a great deal of money and don't actually lead to increased health. Some tests provide the illusion of certainty without actually improving anything. This is doubtless true in schools.

The Dog Needs a New Tail

In 1969 the Harvard psychologist Arthur Jensen published an article in the influential and highly regarded *Harvard Educational Review*.[1] In the paper, Jensen argued that black children were not as intelligent as white children. To support his argument, he presented elegant data from his own lab. In one of his key studies, children were read a list of words (*cat, chair, apple, table, dog,* and so on). After a brief interval, each child was asked to recall the words on the list. (He drew this method from the original intelligence tests. Ever since the French educator Alfred Binet invented them in the nineteenth century, standard IQ tests have taken a person's capacity to recall items from a list or display as a central indicator of intellectual capacity.) And in Jensen's studies white children consistently remembered more items from the list than black children. This happened no matter what kinds of things were on the list (fruit, furniture, tools, vehicles, you name it) or what age group completed the task. Black children didn't seem able to recall as many items as white children. At the time, some felt that Jensen's research had finally pinpointed the reason for apparent differences between black and white children when it came to school performance. How could black children get good grades or do as well in schoolwork if they just weren't as smart?

Needless to say, Jensen's article set off a firestorm of response. Policy makers, educators, and researchers from fields as diverse as biology, genetics, education, and psychology weighed in. Some questioned the method, arguing that the specific tasks Jensen used gave an advantage to white children (based on the idea that black children were intimidated by the setting, or that the task itself required skills more likely to be acquired in school, which white children had greater access to at the time). Many people were simply outraged by Jensen's conclusions; it just seemed morally and humanly repugnant to conclude that black people were not as smart as white people. And quite a few challenged Jensen's basic assumption, that the particular tasks used in his studies really measured intelligence. What made him think, for instance, that the number of words one could recall captured something that as dynamic and complex as smartness? Then, as now, people argued about what it means to be smart, and how we know smartness when we see it. When asked what *he* thought intelligence was, Jensen answered, "Intelligence is whatever it is intelligence tests measure."

Though Jensen's research and his conclusions about race and intelligence were seriously flawed and terribly misguided, he was a smart man and a good scientist. And he was right about one thing: the tests we use often end up defining our reality. For example, most of us make quick intuitive judgments about who is smart and who is not. We base these judgments on all kinds of signs—how funny people are, how good they are at their jobs, how quickly or easily they understand us, and how much they seem to know. You may have thought for years that your cousin John is smarter than your cousin Chris. But if you were to find out that Chris had scored off the charts on an IQ test while John actually had a fairly low score, you'd be hard-pressed to hold on to your previous hunch. Without realizing it, you'd begin revising your impressions of both people. Tests create reality as much as they measure it.

Schools are no different. Everywhere I go I encounter people who quickly distance themselves from the use of standardized tests in schools. This disavowal often cuts across traditional party lines. Nevertheless, most parents, teachers, and local officials find it impossible to ignore the test scores themselves.

My community is a good example. Most of my friends and neighbors in rural western Massachusetts will regularly say standardized tests are limited at best, destructive at worst. Comments range from "Oh, those tests don't tell you anything" to "Standardized testing has ruined the local classrooms." But each year, when the local newspaper publishes the test scores of the region's schools, taxpayers, policy makers, and parents go into a swivet. When they take one glance at a table of numbers, a school that previously seemed rigid, dull, or snooty now is seen as desirable, interesting, and lively. Meanwhile, if a school just a few miles away, where all kinds of interesting things may be happening— theater programs, new courses, a student-run orchard—gets lower-than-expected scores, people begin to wonder whether it needs new leadership, or why they should pay higher taxes for a building renovation.

If test scores sway the way people view a school, they have an even more powerful impact on what happens within the school. When teachers worry too much about test scores, their teaching changes. They focus more on right answers than on good thinking; they tend to zero in on questions that are likely to be on the test, rather than on topics and questions that they deem intellectually important or interesting to the students. Teachers who feel constantly pressured to meet specific assessment standards are often led to worse, not better, teaching practices.

I conducted a study in which we brought teachers into our lab and asked them to carry out a learning activity with a nine-year-old. Some of the teachers were encouraged to make sure that the student with whom they were working finished the provided worksheet by the end of the session. Others were instead encouraged to explore the topic with their student. That simple and fairly subtle contrast in emphasis made all the difference. Teachers who were told to finish a worksheet discouraged the children from asking too many questions or deviating from the plan. On the other hand, teachers who were told to explore the topic encouraged the children to ask questions and try things out. The lesson from all of this is that the way in which we evaluate our students influences what teachers do, and goes a long way toward shaping the process of education.

In another study, I sat in the corner and watched a second-grade language arts lesson unfold. The children were asked to write down a favorite memory. One exuberant little boy watched the teacher as she gave the instructions. His dark brown eyes were sparkling with good cheer, and he looked like he might bounce right out of his chair. Before she had even finished talking, he had begun writing with his number two pencil on the paper she had handed out, which had double-spaced lines already printed on it. He was writing away for several minutes, a little flushed and totally absorbed. The teacher wandered by, looking over each child's shoulder to make sure everyone was on task and following the instructions. He looked up, clearly eager to engage her whenever he could. "Mrs. Lurey, Mrs. Lurey, see? I'm writing about going back to Mexico at Christmas vacation. I'm writing about my uncle's house. We made our own tortillas. We had a lot of parties. And one night there was a big, big fire. Not a good kind. The bad kind."

The teacher interrupted, "Stop right there, Antonio. You're getting a little off track. Why don't you pick something that's a little easier to write about? That sounds like a big story. And this story, well, this story is for practice. In two months, we're going to take some tests. And you'll need to show that you can spell all the words. Make sure you use your punctuation. And don't get lost in the story."

In her eagerness to make sure Antonio was practicing what he needed to for the tests, the teacher gave him feedback that might lead to a better score but certainly wouldn't encourage his love of writing. Moreover, it was probably not likely to make him a better writer. Encouraging a "big story," letting him "get lost in the story," and letting him tell what he cared about would have been the right steps to take in helping Antonio learn to write well. But she felt she had to steer him toward the very concrete and measurable accomplishments that would appear on the test.

If school is a dog, our tests are its tail. And that tail is wagging hard. This wouldn't be a problem if the tests predicted something valuable. It might be worth the constraints the tests impose on children and teachers if the scores predicted something important. Do they?

In the past few years, parents, teachers, and policy makers have furiously debated whether standardized tests should be used to promote or hold back children, fire teachers, and withhold funds from schools. The debate has focused for the most part on whether the tests are being used in unfair ways. But almost no one has publicly questioned a fundamental assumption—that the tests measure something meaningful or predict something significant beyond themselves.

I have reviewed more than three hundred studies of K–12 academic tests. What I have discovered is startling. Most tests used to evaluate students, teachers, and school districts predict almost nothing except the likelihood of achieving similar scores on subsequent tests. I have found virtually no research demonstrating a relationship between those tests and measures of thinking or life outcomes. To grasp what we do and do not (yet) know about standardized tests, we should consider a few essential puzzles: why we find individual differences in test scores (why one child does better or worse than another), what makes a child's test scores go up, and what such improvement could possibly indicate.

Most researchers agree that several non-school-related factors have a big impact on children's performance on academic tests. These factors help explain why, overall, most children's test scores are fairly stable. Children in poverty do less well, all other things being equal, than children from families with adequate incomes. Children who don't hear much language at home are at an academic disadvantage, which is manifested in their test performance, among other places. Children whose parents read a lot do better than children whose parents don't read. And these factors all tend to be bundled together: middle-class children are more likely to have educated parents and hear more language at home than children who grow up in poverty. In other words, some children have a lot of educational advantage compared to others, and this is reflected in their test scores. If you hold all of these non-school-related features of the environment steady—for instance, by comparing only children who come from the same economic background—some children will still do better than others. The remaining difference between children is, to some extent, a function of underlying intelligence. Both home environment and intelligence are quite stable factors. Children who get a higher than average test score in third grade are likely to get a higher than average test score in ninth grade.

But most of us believe that intelligence and family background do not seal a child's fate. We believe that children can learn something in school that gives them knowledge and skills above and beyond what they can acquire on their own. Furthermore, the current faith in testing suggests that we believe that test scores are a good measure of whether children are learning something valuable at school. As we have seen in the news, some classrooms (or even whole schools) have succeeded in boosting children's scores beyond what was predicted by their earlier scores. When children's scores go up, assuming no cheating is involved, does it indicate that a specific teacher or educational practice has helped those children know more and think better than they otherwise would have?

Perhaps, but I have seen no good empirical evidence of this. To show that improved test scores actually indicate a more knowledgeable and skilled child, we need three kinds of evidence. First, we need evidence that when a child scores better than she has in the past, her knowledge or skills extend beyond the specific items on the test. So far, the evidence has not shown this. In many states where children have shown dramatic improvement on the standard tests, the apparent improvement vanishes when they are given a new or different test. As one school principal I know said to me, "One of my teachers reported that her students had particular trouble with questions that involved reading a menu. Her solution was to include menu items in the weeks of schoolwork leading up to the test." It goes without saying that familiarity with menus was not the real problem. What those children needed was not more time practicing menu questions, but instead more skills for reading unfamiliar material, for understanding a new domain by reading about it, and figuring out how to navigate new literary formats. Her students may well have improved on the next round of tests, but that wouldn't necessarily mean they had actually become better readers.

Second, it would be good to know that when children's test scores improve, their academic performance in non-test settings also improves. In other words, we'd need evidence that the teacher whose students regularly get scores better than what would have been predicted by their earlier scores is helping those students become better thinkers and learners more generally. For instance, we'd need to see that children who test better on reading comprehension items also choose more complex books, use books in a more sophisticated way to form opinions, and speak in more literate and authoritative ways. There are virtually no data to show this.

Third, even in the absence of these two kinds of research, it would be good to know that improving a child's test score actually improved his or her life outcome. Research has established that good test scores can *cause* good things to happen; a good score might qualify a student for an enriched academic opportunity or a scholarship at the state university (as it does in Massachusetts). But does an improved score measure some underlying change that augurs well for a child? For instance, if the children in, say, Mrs. Good's fourth-grade class showed more improvement from third grade than the students in Mrs. Bad's fourth-grade class, it would be useful to know if, fifteen years later, Mrs. Good's students had better jobs, did better at their jobs, found more life satisfaction, and were more conscientious voters than children in Mrs. Bad's class. It would be equally important to show that the children in Mrs. Good's class had better life outcomes than the students in Mr. Alsogood's class, where children's scores didn't go up but where other good things were happening (for instance, children were engaged, working hard, and reading a lot). That is, whatever a teacher does to improve students' scores should also predict a better chance at a good life.

So far, there is little strong evidence on any of these important questions. Until we have data showing that improved test scores (at least on the kinds of tests we've been using) actually indicate that students have learned to think well, or that improved test scores predict better life outcomes, we're all willfully looking away from the emperor's nakedness. Are there alternatives?

Several groups across the nation advocate getting rid of school tests altogether. Many of these groups point to the fact that in some places where schools seem to be working very well, they barely use test scores at all. Finland is first among these examples. However, there are two big problems with that argument. First of all, ultimately the way that people know that Finland's schools are so good is, in fact, through test results. Just not local-content-based tests, but rather Program for International Student Assessment (PISA) test scores, which have been used to compare nations. In recent years Finland has gotten some of the highest PISA scores, and the United States has not. So it's not exactly accurate to suggest that the Finns do not use standardized test scores. They do, but perhaps not to the extent that we do. Second, of course, the size and demographics of Finland render it nearly incomparable to our nation in terms of the goals and challenges students face.

I'm not suggesting that the many and varied communities within the United States shouldn't be able to hold their schools accountable in some fairly objective way that people can understand. It certainly doesn't make sense to expect all parents to be able to evaluate the teaching and learning that are going on in a school merely by visiting it, any more than we can expect most people to understand whether a particular hospital has good surgical practices or is using the best methods for diagnosing disease.

In fact, the comparison between schools and hospitals is a telling one. In the past ten years, doctors have engaged in an intriguing debate about medical practice. Jerome Groopman has argued that doctors need to deliberate, consider alternatives, and think through each case in an open-minded way.[2] Atul Gawande, on the other hand, has argued that doctors (and hospitals more generally) need to systematize things: use checklists as a way of guarding against human error, build automatic habits (like handwashing) into their daily practice, and use quantitative data to evaluate how they're doing.[3] It is tempting to apply this same type of thinking to schools. There are many parallels between hospitals and schools, and between doctors and teachers. Both are in the business of improving people's lives. The best doctors and the best teachers depend on a certain alchemical blend of good scientific data and intuition. Both must be skilled technicians as well as good with human beings. If you discovered you had to have an operation on your brain and someone told you that you might have to choose between someone who was really smart, someone who was well trained, and someone who had great hands, you'd be justifiably upset, since you'd want all three. Choosing one of those attributes over another would seem unacceptable. Similarly, it's not unreasonable to want teachers who are smart, who have had good training, and who have some intuitive feel for being with kids.

Given the intriguing parallels between medicine and education, it would seem reasonable to try to compare the way we evaluate the two institutions. The Cleveland Clinic, which is considered one of the best hospitals in the United States, uses 115 metrics to evaluate its performance. But doctors use those metrics to figure out how they are falling short, and to devise ways to improve. The metrics don't guide people's choice of a hospital. Instead, according to Toby Cosgrove, head of the Cleveland Clinic, people choose a hospital based on informal reports of its reputation (from neighbors, magazines, and the like), whether the staff is polite, whether it smells good, and whether people look organized. Often the way they are treated at the front desk matters as much to them as the quality of the medical treatment they receive. But overall, health professionals and patients have the same big picture in mind. Everyone uses the same overarching measure of a hospital's success: the number of patients who leave the hospital alive, and the number of patients who are healthier when they leave than when they entered.

Hospitals exist to fix problems. If no one got sick, they would disappear. Schools, on the other hand, are not intended to fix a problem. Schools are supposed to provide something good, helping people acquire knowledge and abilities beyond what comes naturally. Put another way, patients come to hospitals unwell and for the most part unhappy. Children come to school for the most part intact and with all kinds of strengths (even children who come from poverty or a difficult home often have intelligence, a cheerful outlook on life, an urge to do well, or a real interest in something). The point here is that, unlike hospitals, there is no simple or neat general metric that parents can use to evaluate schools. For all the reasons I've identified, test scores are not particularly useful and are often misleading, and most parents wouldn't find a visit to the school all that useful either.

And yet a community has the right to know if its school is not doing a good job. State and federal governments also have the right to know, since they bear some financial responsibility for schools. Most important, of course, teachers and their principals should want data to help them see if they are reaching their goals. The idea that teachers just "know" when a kid is learning is as ridiculous as thinking that hospitals just "know" whether they are using the best possible procedures.

Recently I sat with a group of kind, skilled, and well-intentioned elementary school teachers. They were railing against the current standardized tests, as teachers so often do when they gather these days. One teacher who was in her late fifties and had taught all her life said, "I don't need these tests to tell me when a child has learned to read. I just know it in my gut." Well, she's wrong there. Research has shown again and again how wrong our gut is when it comes to estimating our own efficacy and contribution: when married people were asked to estimate their contribution to various aspects of domestic life, in most couples both the husband and the wife calculated that they contributed more than 50 percent, which clearly is not possible. Most of us tend to see our own contribution as greater than anyone else's, and most of us tend to think we are doing a better job than we really are. And after all, when children are measured for what they have learned, teachers have a powerful if unconscious motivation to see that their students have done well. When a student doesn't learn or improve, it's only natural for a teacher to feel that he or she has not been effective. Research has shown that it is completely human and fairly universal to twist reality around in order to make oneself feel good and competent. We fool ourselves, and teachers are no different.

Ideally, everyone would benefit from objective measures of children's learning in schools. The answer is not to abandon testing, but to measure the things we most value, and find good ways to measure those things. How silly to measure a child's ability to parse a sentence or solve certain kinds of math problems if in fact those measures don't predict anything important about the child or lead to better teaching practices. The only notable feature of the tests we currently use is that they are relatively easy to administer to every child in every school, are easy to score, and appear (though are not really) easy to understand. But expediency should not be our main priority when it comes to schools.

When you hear people debate the use of tests in schools, the talk usually assumes that the only alternative to the current approach is no testing at all. But nothing could be further from the truth. Why not test the things we value, and test them in a way that provides us with an accurate picture of what children really do, not what they can do under the most constrained circumstances after the most constrained test preparation? Nor should this be very difficult. After all, in the past fifty years economists and psychologists have found ways to measure things as subtle and dynamic as the mechanisms that explain when and why we give in to impulse, the forces that govern our moral choices, and the thought processes that underlie unconscious stereotyping.

So why not measure the qualities and processes that are important to children's lives in the here and now and which lead to good things in the future? The rest of this chapter discusses a fairly short list of abilities and dispositions that children should acquire or improve upon—and therefore should be measured—while in school. The first few elements are more traditionally academic, though the emphasis is less on a long laundry list of specific skills and more on core intellectual habits. The others are capacities that have been ignored by the world of measurement.

A Note on Measurement

The value of traditional assessments rests on the assumption that what a child can do under the very specific conditions of timed paper-and-pencil tests captures some more general and stable characteristic of that child. Most people are familiar with the ways in which performance on these tests can underestimate a child's ability, such as when the child is nervous taking tests, doesn't think well working under strict time constraints, or thinks in unconventional ways that are not tapped by the specific questions asked or the rigid way the tests are scored. But these tests are misleading in another way that gets less attention. A child who is well schooled and eager to shine in such a setting shows what he or she can do when asked, but this doesn't necessarily tell you what that child will do in everyday life. Children who can answer math questions correctly don't necessarily use math in everyday life to solve problems; research has shown that even those most adept at school algebra often fail to use such algebraic thinking when solving everyday problems such as finding the location of an address, figuring out the logistics of traveling a certain distance at a certain time, or calculating how to divvy up a shared reward on the basis of different amounts of labor. Children who can answer short questions about a passage of text don't necessarily read to gain new information, to help them make decisions, or to expand their understanding of life. Many of the measures I am proposing instead depend on getting what are called periodic samples of children's behavior.

Video data have the advantage of showing what children and teachers actually do, not what they can do when they know they are being evaluated. To make this work the way it does in good research, the samples have to be gathered on an unpredictable (random) schedule, and the data collection has to be fairly unobtrusive. This could be relatively easy to do given our current technological capabilities. Every classroom could have several cameras installed, and these could be set to collect data at a variety of times through the year. These data would then need to be analyzed by trained coders.

There are some obstacles to overcome if we want to use such data to evaluate children and schools. Most people who hear this proposal object in one of two ways. Some have a somewhat reflexive fear that such cameras would automatically become the tool of Big Brother—that by videotaping children we are either invading their privacy or the teachers' privacy. However, classrooms should not be private; they should be public. Increasingly, law enforcement officials videotape their interrogations, and hospitals have recorded various kinds of procedures and interactions between staff and patients for a while now. Moreover, recording what goes on in classrooms would be far less intrusive or potentially destructive than the vast amount of data currently collected online without anyone really knowing what is being collected and for what purposes. The videotaped data would, it's true, have to be handled carefully—seen only by trained educational evaluators, and then destroyed or archived, just as research data are. The potential richness of such data and the clearer picture they would give us of what children are really doing in school are benefits that far outweigh the potential privacy risks, all of which are as easy to manage as those in any other data collection system.

The second objection people make is that this would be a costly and cumbersome approach to assessment. But given the incredible expense of the current approach, in which virtually every child is tested every year, this seems like a ridiculous concern. Compared to the construction, dissemination, and scoring of comprehensive paper-and-pencil tests, there is nothing inherently more expensive about collecting and coding random samples of video footage. One key feature of the system I am suggesting is that it depends, like good research, on representative samples rather than on testing every child every year. We'd use less data, to better effect, and free up the hours, days, and weeks now spent on standardized test prep and the tests themselves, time that could be spent on real teaching and learning.

Finally, there is one additional benefit to using such video data. The only way to game this system would actually improve classroom practice. Imagine a third-grade teacher who knows that her class will, at unexpected times throughout the school year, be observed and that coders will be looking for, among other things, signs of peer collaboration and sustained conversation. In order to look good in the footage, she encourages lots of collaboration and conversation throughout the day. This, it seems, would be a good kind of "teaching to the test."

Measuring Essential Abilities and Dispositions

Reading

Every child should be able to read by the end of elementary school. Just as important, every child should be reading on a regular basis, turning to books and other written material for pleasure and for information. What does it mean to be able to read? It means having the ability to read an essay or book and understand it well enough to use the information in some practical way, or to talk about it with another person.

When children can read and do read, their language and thinking are different. One way to measure reading, then, is to take a close look at their language and thinking. For example, using recordings of children's everyday speech, developmental psychologists can calculate two important indicators of intellectual functioning: the grammatical complexity of their sentences and the size of their working vocabularies (not the words they circle during a test, but the ones they use in their real lives). Why not do the same in schools? Additionally, we could employ a written version of this method, collecting random samples of children's essays and stories for analysis.

Psychologists have also found that a good indication of a person's literacy level is his or her ability to identify the names of real authors amidst names of nonauthors. In other words, a person who knows that Junot Díaz and J.K. Rowling are published authors, while Richard Castle is not, is more literate than the one who cannot identify the real writers. We could periodically administer such a test to children to find out how much they have read as opposed to which isolated skills they have been practicing for a test.

When children recount a story that they have read or that has been read to them, it provides all kinds of information about their narrative skill, an essential component of literacy. We could give students a book and then have them talk with a trained examiner about what they read; the oral reconstruction could be analyzed for evidence of their narrative comprehension.

Measuring children's basic ability to read something and understand it, as well as the frequency with which they actually turn to the written word for pleasure or knowledge, should not be complicated, nor need it be tested again and again. Schools and children would be a lot better off if we identified a basic quality and quantity of reading. Once that benchmark was reached, other things could be tracked.

Inquiry
Children are born wanting to find things out. But schools have, by and large, done little to build on this valuable impulse. In fact, when children get to school, they ask fewer questions, explore

less often and with less intensity, and become less curious. One of the great ironies of our educational system is that it seems to squelch the impulse most essential to learning new things and to pursuing scientific discovery and invention. The good news is that researchers have developed excellent methods for measuring children's interest in finding things out, as well as their ability to investigate in increasingly deliberate, thorough, and precise ways. Here there are several ways we might measure a child's disposition to inquire. We can easily record the number of questions the child asks during a given stretch of time. We can also rate those questions: Does the child ask questions that can be answered with data? Does the child persist in asking questions when he or she doesn't get the answer right away? Does the child seem to use a range of techniques to get answers (asking someone else, going online, manipulating objects, and looking at things, to name a few important strategies)?

Researchers have found that the way a student critiques a simple science experiment shows whether he or she understands the idea of controlling variables, which is a key component in all science work. To assess scientific skills, children could read about a scientific experiment or look at a scientific poster (the kind used by researchers and by students during science fairs) and then explain how they would improve upon it. Children's explanations of experiments have already been coded by researchers, so figuring out how to evaluate such student responses would not be hard at all.

Flexible Thinking and the Use of Evidence

One of the most important capacities to be gained by going to school is the ability to think about a situation in several different ways. This has already been measured in college students. Why not measure it in younger children? Students could write essays in response to a prompt such as "Choose something you are good at, and describe to your reader how you do it." That would allow each student to draw on an area of expertise, assess his or her ability, describe a task logically, and convey real information and substance. A prompt of "Write a description of yourself from a friend's (or enemy's) point of view" would help gauge the ability to understand the perspectives of others, another invaluable skill.

Conversation

Conversations are key to achieving many of the other goals I've discussed, but they're also important in and of themselves. And they're not hard to measure. Researchers have been analyzing conversations and the development of conversational skill for many years. Methods include looking at how long a conversation is (for example, how many sentences are uttered, how many words are used, how much time the conversation takes), how many turns each speaker takes, how many of these turns are in response to what was just said, how many topics are discussed, how full or deep the coverage of a topic is, and how attuned each speaker is to what has just been said. Outside coders could code children's conversations for a number of characteristics: turns taken, depth of topic, amount of information exchanged, points of view articulated, and number of agreements and disagreements within the conversation. Analyses could also look at things such as the percentage of students in a given classroom who participate in conversations (to make sure that it's not just one student or a small group doing all the talking). These analyses would have to take stock of what kinds of things children discuss, and in what settings.

It would also be good to consider the role of the teacher in such conversations. Many studies have shown that adults play a crucial role in the acquisition of conversational skills. When researchers have recorded conversations between children and their parents at home, they have found that many parents talk frequently with their children, answering and asking questions, leading their children to expand and enrich their answers, and using the conversations to learn what their children are thinking about and what they know. Parents also use the conversations to offer their children new information about the world, as well as to teach (albeit without consciously trying to) the art of conversation. However, not all families are the same in this regard, and research has also shown that children living in poverty are much less likely to hear and be part of such rich exchanges at home. This makes it all the more essential for teachers to encourage a lot of discussion and verbal exchange at school.

While parents intuitively know how to encourage and nurture dialogue, it cannot be assumed that teachers will be equally intuitive. Encouraging conversation in a classroom setting is a whole different ball game. It's not easy to make room for children to talk to one another, much less find time to engage in conversations with individual students or small groups. It's not always easy to help a child expand his or her linguistic or narrative repertoire, especially when the teacher and child come from different oral traditions. Teachers are given scant training about how to encourage, expand, and deeper children's conversations. Schools of education offer lots of courses on curriculum planning, reading strategies, assessment, and classroom management, but I have seen few places where teachers deliberately reflect on or practice ways to have real conversations with their students. It would be easy to assume that teachers, by definition, are naturally good at this. But that is not the case.

I recently sat in the back of a large, pleasant room watching a seasoned teacher trainer lead a workshop for elementary school teachers on constructing scenes with small blocks to help children understand stories they had read. The workshop leader began to explain how to get students to talk to one another about their constructions: "Ask each child, in turn, to tell the others what they made, and what book it comes from. When they're done, don't praise them; this isn't about you. Simply say, 'Thanks for telling us.' As they go, some of the others will pipe up and make comments or ask questions. Don't let them speak directly to one another. They often ask the wrong kinds of questions. Instead, if a child wants to know something about one of the other students' constructions, they should ask you the question. Then you can translate, turning it into a good question. You can then say to the child who has been explaining her work, 'So-and-so wants to know why you chose to make only the outside of the park and not the inside.' Make sure you are the go-between." Needless to say, such rigid control is not likely to encourage rich dialogues or give the children much chance to talk to one another about their ideas.

If teachers knew that their students' conversations were valuable and that they and their students were being measured by their conversations, they might get more help learning how to scaffold or enrich children's talk. And unlike the kinds of "teaching to the test" we have come to know, which diminish a child's educational experience, this kind of "teaching to the test" would improve children's educational experiences day in and day out.

Collaborations

Vida had two young sons, both enrolled at the public school in her suburban community on the West Coast. Her older son, Quinn, was short, like his dad. But when you're nine years old, being shorter than the other boys is a liability. Quinn wore glasses for nearsightedness, and with his mom's help he had chosen hip thick-rimmed glasses that had a band around the back to keep them in place; they made him look a little odd, almost as though he were wearing swimming goggles. He was a dreamer, happiest when he was lost in a book. He was reluctant to do sports and unsure of himself on the playground. He began to complain to his mother that he didn't really have friends at school, and many mornings he didn't want to go. Vida wasn't sure how to help him. Then he began to tell her that lunch was the worst. A little boy named Sean, popular, athletic, and in command, had his own special table. All the kids referred to it as "Sean's table," and kids could only sit there by invitation. The children in Sean's inner circle had permanent chairs at the table. Quinn wasn't in the inner circle; he wasn't even in the outer circle. Not knowing where to sit was making him miserable.

Though this kind of story appears again and again in parenting magazines, and every group of parents has shared similar tales of social woe, the issue should be an educational one, not simply a parental ache. Teachers can help children like Quinn learn how to navigate their social settings, and helping children with this skill is surely just as valuable as teaching them to add, subtract, and spell. But perhaps more important, teachers can help kids like Sean learn to resist the perfectly natural but undesirable impulse to exclude and dominate others in social settings. In order to do this, teachers need to devote time each day to guiding children through the jungle of social interaction.

In a 2000 study Canadian researchers placed video cameras in a school playground in order to find out how children behave toward one another when outside the classroom.[4] Their cameras revealed that bullying incidents occurred about 4.5 times per hour. In addition, other children typically stood by and watched the bullying unfold. Studies such as this one show that being kind to one another and standing up for others does not come naturally. Just as Freud pointed out in his classic work *Civilization and Its Discontents*, development is a long, treacherous path of learning to suppress one's selfish hunger for satisfaction in order to become part of a cordial and cooperative group.[5] Children must learn to work side by side, to compromise, to include one another, and to defend one another. If communal life were a priority in school, children would acquire habits of collaboration, inclusion, and conflict resolution. But to measure this, you'd have to see children in their natural settings.

Here again, videotaped material, gathered periodically and on a random schedule, would show how often children help one another and how often they hurt one another. It would also be possible to assess teachers' efforts to help children acquire essential social skills. For instance, the data would reveal how frequently children are given opportunities to collaborate. In addition, coders could identify what kinds of encouragement and guidance teachers provide to help children learn how to work with one another. It would be possible to evaluate the quality and quantity of guidance given about social problem solving.

Such data might be supplemented by other information. A whole range of simple tasks reveals how aggressive children are, how they interpret various social interactions, and how they think about solving specific problems within a group. For example, some psychologists invite children to play an online game and measure the number of aggressive moves each child makes during the game. In one particularly clever and informative experiment, researchers invited small groups of children into the lab and gave them one very attractive toy to play with, watching to see the various ways the children shared the toy. In another version of this, researchers asked a small group of children to solve a difficult task and then assessed their collaborative skills. Why not periodically administer such behavioral tests as a way of seeing if particular styles of classrooms or schools help children become more skilled at collaboration?

One of the most robust findings in developmental psychology is that children learn how to treat one another by watching the way adults treat them and treat each other. This is no less true for teachers than it is for parents. Yet few teacher-training programs emphasize the informal ways in which teachers behave. Nor do principals and superintendents attend much to how teachers treat children throughout the day, or to how they interact with other teachers.

When parents ask me what to look for when visiting a new school, I always tell them to hang out in the hallways, looking at what is on the walls, listening to what teachers say to students as they pass by, and watching what teachers say to one another. If there's one thing we know, it's that collaboration and kindness emerge in a given setting only when such values permeate the group. The habits of kindness and teamwork need time, effort, and attention to develop. In other words, just as it's important to assess whether children seem to be getting more skilled at helping each other and working together, and are more inclined to do so, it's important to assess the ways in which teachers are making such collaboration possible. It's true that teachers might prep kids for such assessments, but in this case the prep itself might actually be of educational value.

Engagement

In order to find out whether children are regularly absorbed in what they are learning, they need to be assessed in naturalistic settings. The important thing to find out is whether children are provided with opportunities to become fully absorbed in various kinds of activity, at least some of the time. It is also essential to assess whether, given those opportunities, they concentrate on what they are doing and are energized by it.

Once again, segments of recorded activity from a classroom would reveal how many children, in a given stretch of time, seem absorbed in something and for how long. As noted earlier, the educational philosopher Harry Brighouse has suggested that the ability to think about something for twenty minutes at a time (sustained focus) may be one of the most powerful cognitive skills we acquire in school. Needless to say, some children seem to have great stores of such focus from the get-go, while others find the road to sustained concentration long and nearly impossible to travel. But the measures I am arguing for here are not meant to show which child is better at concentrating and which child is worse. Instead, they are meant to ensure that the majority of children are meeting a basic benchmark. We don't need to insist that children become ever more absorbed (in other words, children and schools don't need to get higher marks each year). Nor should we hold back children who never seem as engaged as their buddies. Instead the assessment should simply show that an individual child does become deeply immersed in one thing or another periodically. Similarly, the assessments can show whether a given classroom is providing ample enough opportunities for immersion. Thus the engagement measures, like others described here, provide proof of critical benchmarks for children and for classrooms.

Well-Being

In his enduringly wonderful children's book *Many Moons*, James Thurber describes a princess who is dying of sadness because she longs for the moon.[6] Her father, the king, calls in all his most eminent advisors, who suggest elaborate methods for getting the moon in order to give it to the princess. None of the advice works. In sadness and desperation, the king commands the court jester to come cheer him up. When the jester finds out why the king is so sad, he suggests they simply ask the princess how to solve the problem. Lo and behold, the princess tells the jester just where the moon is, what it is made of, and how they can get it for her.

I have argued that first and foremost children should be acquiring a sense of well-being in school. So why not ask them periodically how they feel? Questions might probe what they are working on that they care about, how often they like being there, whether they feel known by adults in the school, and how much of the time they feel interested in at least some of what they are doing. Economists and psychologists have shown that people are pretty reliable when it comes to telling us how happy they are. Why not use this metric in evaluating our schools?

These are just a few of the methods that would capture a child's educational progress more effectively than the typical paper-and-pencil tests, which tend to show how much a child has been rehearsing certain content areas. Moreover, the metrics I've proposed directly assess the capacities that actually matter in life outside of the testing room.

We don't need to exhaustively track every child every year in order to monitor how schools are doing. Just as researchers often use a randomly selected group to provide a window onto the larger population, we need to test only carefully gathered representative samples from all the classes within a few grades. More and more measurement has not proved to be useful in other parts of life (medicine, for instance). And it's not useful in educational settings. Instead, we need to check in on classrooms, to ensure that they are encouraging certain core dispositions, and do simple assessments to make sure that children are progressing toward mastering a few important basic abilities. We don't need exhaustive census-like data on our students or on our schools. Instead we need an empirical snapshot of a school. By approaching assessment this way, we'd free up students and teachers to do more meaningful work.

AFTERWORD

Not long ago, I met with an old friend who is a fifth-grade teacher. She is forty-eight years old. She's been at it a long time, and she loves her classroom and the children in it. But in recent years she's felt worn down by requirements that seriously hamper her and her students. She told me that recently she was so fed up, she decided she would go wild and make January the month when she just did what she wanted with her class. She put away all the regular worksheets and long lists of curricular goals given to her by the state. She stashed away the sheets with detailed information about her children's reading and math scores. She hid the book telling her which science units she had to cover by June. Instead she decided her students would do only three things that month: (1) They'd read as much as they wanted, whatever they wanted. She'd read aloud to them, they'd read to themselves, and sometimes one of them would read to friends. (2) They'd eat lunch together in the classroom, where it was peaceful and they could hear one another talk. And (3) they'd build a time machine, something her students had wanted to do all year.

To prepare, she brought in lots and lots of books. Some were hers, and some she bought at thrift shops and tag sales. She brought in music to play at lunchtime. And she learned every-thing she could about time travel—science as well as science fic-tion. Late in January, I stopped by the classroom. Two boys were huddled at the computer, having found their way to a website about quantum physics. They were reading an essay about black holes and the theory of relativity. Next to them was a piece of paper on which they were taking notes and scribbling various models showing how the time machine might work. They were arguing over the calculations they needed to make so that the time machine would reflect theoretical physicist Stephen Hawk-ing's explanation. The bell rang, and the teacher announced that it was time to put things away for recess.

The boys were still hunched over the computer, eyes glued to the screen. One whispered urgently to the other, "Keep your head down. Maybe she won't notice us. Then we can stay in and figure this out."

"Ssshh," the other boy answered, "I'm reading. Just tell her whatever you want. I know we're gonna get this. We've gotta get this."

In all my years of visiting schools, watching children, and meeting with teachers, I have seen students discover a love of books, realize that it feels wonderful to work hard toward a goal they've set for themselves, and experience the joy and satisfac-tion of depending on one another. I've also been to schools where teachers get to talk to each other every week about their teaching, and where serious conversations and inquiry are at the core of the curriculum. Many pieces of what I have proposed in this book are already happening. We don't need a wholesale reinvention of ed-ucation, as some have suggested. Nor do we need to abandon the idea that children can learn things in school that will help them do well at a job. Instead, we can reframe the whole enterprise so that the important things happening in school take center stage, getting the time, energy, and attention they require. Meanwhile, many of the destructive features that drag down teachers and children alike will become unnecessary.

It is up to governments and policy makers to ensure that every child has access to safe, reasonably staffed schools. It is up to educators to educate—to help children become thoughtful, engaged, and connected to others, so that when they graduate they will be well on their way to a pot of gold worth having.

NOTES

Prologue

1. Jonathan Swift, *A Modest Proposal* (1729; New York: Dover Publications, 1996).

2. Mark Bauerlein, "The Paradox of Classroom Boredom," *Education Week*, August 6, 2013.

One: The Money Trail

1. Andrew Carnegie, *The Autobiography of Andrew Carnegie* (New York: PublicAffairs, 2011), 29.

2. *Oxford Dictionary of National Biography*, "Andrew Carnegie," www.oxforddnb.com/public/index-content.html.

3. David Nasaw, *Andrew Carnegie* (New York: Penguin, 2007).

4. Carnegie, *Autobiography*, 12.

5. Ibid., 21.

6. Ibid., 33.

7. Nasaw, *Andrew Carnegie*, 12.

8. Carnegie, *Autobiography*, 4.

9. John Spargo, *The Bitter Cry of the Children* (New York: Macmillan, 1909), 127.

10. The photograph is part of a collection at the Library of Congress, Frances Benjamin Johnston, "United States Indian School, Carlisle, Pennsylvania," 1901–3, www.loc.gov/pictures /collection/coll/item/86706686/.

11. "Schools and Teachers," *New York Times*, March 27, 1901.

12. "New York City's Schools and What They Cost," *New York Times*, September 13, 1908.

13. John Dewey, *The School and Society and the Child and the Curriculum* (Chicago: University of Chicago Press, 2013).

14. John Dewey, *Democracy and Education* (New York: Free Press, 1916), 228.

15. U.S. Department of Education, *A Nation at Risk*, April 1983, www2.ed.gov/pubs/NatAtRisk/risk.html.

16. Thomas Friedman, "It's the PQ and the CQ as Much as the IQ," *New York Times*, January 29, 2013.

17. Ibid.

18. Diane Ravitch, *The Death and Life of the Great American School System: How Testing and Choice Are Undermining Education* (New York: Basic Books, 2011).

19. Benno C. Schmidt Jr., "The Edison Project's Plan to Redefine Public Education," *Educational Leadership* 52, no. 1 (September 1994): 61–64.

20. Somini Sengupta, "Edison Project Gets Aid to Open New Schools," *New York Times*, May 27, 1998.

Two: How Money Impoverishes Education

1. Rudolph Flesch, *Why Johnny Can't Read, and What You Can Do About It* (1955; New York: William Morrow, 1986).

2. Diana Jean Schemo, "In War over Teaching Reading, a U.S.-Local Clash," *New York Times*, March 9, 2007.

3. Frank Smith, *Understanding Reading: A Psycholinguistic Analysis of Reading and Learning to Read* (New York: Routledge, 1994).

4. Mark R. Lepper and David Green, "Turning Play into Work: Effects of Adult Surveillance and Extrinsic Rewards on Children's Intrinsic Motivation," *Journal of Personality and Social Psychology* 31, no. 3 (1975): 479–86.

5. Elliot Aronson, "The Theory of Cognitive Dissonance: A Current Perspective," *Advances in Experimental Social Psychology* 41 (1969): 1–34.

6. Jennifer Medina, "Schools Plan to Pay Cash for Marks," *New York Times*, June 19, 2007.

7. Ann Brown, "Transforming Schools into Communities of Thinking and Learning About Serious Matters," *American Psychologist* 52, no. 4 (997): 399–413.

8. Maureen Nolan, "New Schedules for Syracuse Elementary Schools Don't Set Aside Time for Recess," *Post-Standard* (Syracuse, NY), September 8, 2012.

9. Carol Dweck, *Mindset: The New Psychology of Success* (New York: Random House, 2006).

Three: Rich or Poor, It's Good to Have Money

1. Robert H. Bradley and Robert F. Corwyn, "Socioeconomic Status and Child Development," *Annual Review of Psychology* 53, no. 1 (2002): 371–99; Gary W. Evans and Pilyoung Kim, "Childhood Poverty, Chronic Stress, Self-Regulation and Coping," *Child Development Perspectives* 7, no. 1 (2013): 43–48; Gary W. Evans and Pilyoung Kim, "Childhood Poverty and Young Adults' Allostatic Load: The Mediating Role of Childhood Cumulative Risk Exposure," *Psychological Science* 23, no. 9 (2012): 979–83.

2. David L. Kirp, *The Sandbox Investment: The Preschool Movement and Kids-First Politics* (Cambridge, MA: Harvard University Press, 2009).

3. Bridget K. Hamre and Robert C. Pianta, "Early Teacher-Child Relationships and the Trajectory of Children's School Outcomes Through Eighth Grade," *Child Development* 72, no. 2 (2001): 625–38.

4. Daniel Kahneman, Alan B. Krueger, David Schkade, Norbert Schwarz, and Arthur A. Stone, "Would You Be Happier If You Were Richer? A Focusing Illusion," *Science* 312, no. 5782 (2006): 1908–10; Daniel Kahneman and Alan B. Krueger, "Developments in the Measurement of Subjective Well-Being," *Journal of Economic Perspectives* 20, no. 1 (2006): 3–24.

5. Richard A. Easterlin, "Income and Happiness: Towards a Unified Theory," *Economic Journal* 111, no. 473 (2001): 465–84.

6. John F. Helliwell, Richard Layard, and Jeffrey Sachs, eds., *World Happiness Report 2013* (New York: UN Sustainable Developmental Solutions Network, 2013).

7. Tim Kasser and Aaron Ahuvia, "Materialistic Values and Well-Being in Business Students," *European Journal of Social Psychology* 32, no. 1 (2002): 137–46.

8. James E. Burroughs and Aric Rindfleisch, "Materialism and Well-Being: A Conflicting Values Perspective," *Journal of Consumer Research* 29, no. 3 (2002): 348–70.

9. Abraham Harold Maslow, "A Theory of Human Motivation," *Psychological Review* 50, no. 4 (1943): 370.

Four: How Happiness Enriches Schools

1. Nel Noddings, *Happiness and Education* (Cambridge: Cambridge University Press, 2003); Harry Brighouse, *On Education* (New York: Routledge, 2005); Martin E.P. Seligman, *Flourish: A Visionary New Understanding of Happiness and Well-Being* (New York: Simon & Schuster, 2012); Ed Diener and Martin E.P. Seligman, "Beyond Money: Toward an Economy of Well-Being," *Psychological Science in the Public Interest* 5, no. 1 (2004):

1–31; Daniel Gilbert, *Stumbling on Happiness* (New York: Random House, 2009).

2. Joseph E. Stiglitz, Amartya Sen, and Jean-Paul Fitoussi, *Mismeasuring Our Lives: Why GDP Doesn't Add Up* (New York: The New Press, 2010).

3. Mihaly Csikszentmihalyi, *Creativity: Flow and the Psychology of Discovery and Invention* (New York: HarperPerennial, 1997).

4. Jerome S. Bruner, *The Process of Education* (Cambridge, MA: Harvard University Press, 1960).

5. Ann Brown, "Transforming Schools into Communities of Thinking and Learning About Serious Matters," *American Psychologist* 52, no. 4 (997): 399–413.

6. Erik H. Erikson, *Childhood and Society* (New York: W.W. Norton, 1993).

7. William Damon, *The Path to Purpose: Helping Our Children Find Their Calling in Life* (New York: Simon & Schuster, 2008).

8. Jerry Stanley, *Children of the Dust Bowl: The True Story of the School at Weedpatch Camp* (New York: Random House, 1993).

9. Susan Engel, *The Hungry Mind: The Origins of Curiosity* (Cambridge, MA: Harvard University Press, 2015).

10. Ibid.

11. Andrew Shtulman, "Epistemic Similarities Between Students' Scientific and Supernatural Beliefs," *Journal of Educational Psychology* 105, no. 1 (2013): 199–212.

12. Bruner, *Process of Education*.

13. Lev S. Vygotsky, *Mind in Society: The Development of Higher Psychological Processes* (Cambridge, MA: Harvard University Press, 1978).

Five: A Blueprint for Well-Being

1. Esmé Raji Codell, *Educating Esmé: Diary of a Teacher's First Year* (Chapel Hill, NC: Algonquin Books, 2001).

2. Betty Hart and Todd R. Risley, *Meaningful Differences in the Everyday Experience of Young American Children* (Baltimore: Paul H. Brookes, 1995).

3. James Thurber, "A Curb in the Sky," *New Yorker*, November 28, 1931, 18.

4. Catherine E. Snow and Paola Uccelli, "The Challenge of Academic Language," in *The Cambridge Handbook of Literacy*, ed. David R. Olson and Nancy Torrance (New York: Cambridge University Press, 2009), 112–33.

5. Joyce Carol Oates, "Deep Reader: Rebecca Mead's 'My Life in Middlemarch,'" *New York Times Book Review*, January 23, 2014.

6. Laura Lippman, "By the Book," *New York Times Book Review*, February 13, 2014.

7. Codell, *Educating Esmé*.

8. Elliot Aronson and Shelley Patnoe, *The Jigsaw Classroom: Building Cooperation in the Classroom* (New York: Longman Press, 1997).

9. Theodore R. Sizer, *Horace's Compromise: The Dilemma of the American High School* (1984; New York: Houghton Mifflin Harcourt, 2004).

Six: What We Should Measure

1. Arthur R. Jensen, "How Much Can We Boost IQ and Scholastic Achievement?" *Harvard Educational Review* 39, no. 1 (1969): 1–123.

2. Jerome Groopman, *How Doctors Think* (New York: Houghton Mifflin, 2007).

3. Atul Gawande, *Better: A Surgeon's Notes on Performance* (New York: Metropolitan Books, 2007).

4. Wendy M. Craig, Debra Pepler, and Rona Atlas, "Observations of Bullying in the Playground and in the Classroom," *School Psychology International* 21, no. 1 (2000): 22–36.

5. Sigmund Freud, *Civilization and Its Discontents* (1930; New York: W.W. Norton, 2005).

6. James Thurber, *Many Moons* (New York: Harcourt Brace, 1943).

INDEX

"active" learning, 21

adults, knowing and being known by

Carnegie's experiences of learning from relatives, 12, 14

as core element of a school designed to promote well-being and happiness, 159–61

agency (self-efficacy)

and engagement, 74, 103

and executive function, 45, 74

and mastery, 123

offering children autonomy and freedom to make choices, 164–65

American education of mid-nineteenth-century and early twentieth-century, 15–22, 109

and child labor laws, 17, 109–10, 155

city schools, 17–22

industrialization and shift from family work to factory labor, 15–17, 109–10, 155

progressive education movement, 20–22

school population increases, 17–18

specialized curricula for immigrants, working-class, and students of color, 18–20

vocational schools and work preparation, 19–20, 21–22

American Indian schools, early twentieth-century, 18–19

Apted, Michael, 48

Aristotle, 1, 117, 126

Aronson, Elliot, 64–65

art education programs, 76

artwork in schools, 136

autodidacts. *See* teaching oneself new things (ability to learn on one's own)

Bauerlein, Mark, 8
Bertsch, Liz, 100–104
Binet, Alfred, 56, 172
The Bitter Cry of the Children
    (Spargo), 16–17
boredom in the classroom, 8–9,
    47, 114
Brighouse, Harry, 93, 120,
    194–95
Brown, Ann, 71, 103–4, 128
Brown v. Board of Education
    (1954), 150
Bruner, Jerome, 103, 124
bullying and anti-bullying
    measures, 68–69, 126–27,
    163–64, 192–93
Bush, George H. W., 32
Bush, George W., 27–28,
    53–54
business interests in schools,
    32–34, 43
  Edison Schools, 33–34
  marketplace mentalities and
    paying children to learn,
    66–67
  Ravitch on, 32–33

Carlisle Indian School
    (Pennsylvania), 18–19
Carnegie, Andrew, 11–15, 20, 27,
    37–38, 109
Center for Teaching and
    Learning at the University
    of Oregon, 55–56
charter schools, 40, 43–45
  business interests in, 32–34, 43
  Edison Project, 33–34
  Ravitch and, 32–33
  test scores as measurements of
    success, 24, 43

The Child and the Curriculum
    (Dewey), 21
child labor laws, early
    twentieth-century, 17,
    109–10, 155
China, 29
Civilization and Its Discontents
    (Freud), 192
Cleveland Clinic, 181
Codell, Esmé, 137, 149
cognitive dissonance theory
  and children's collaboration
    in racially-integrated jigsaw
    classrooms, 151
  and effects of value placed on
    wealth, 86
  and role of rewards and
    incentives, 64–66
collaboration, cooperation, and
    getting along with other
    people, 68–71, 126–29,
    150–53, 191–94
  anti-bullying measures and
    techniques for helping
    children get along, 68–69,
    126–27, 163–64, 192–93
  as component of happiness, 93,
    108, 129
  as core element of a school
    designed to promote
    well-being and happiness,
    150–53
  effects of academic
    competition on, 69–70
  example of a school garden
    project, 152–53
  group work, 70–71, 128,
    151–53
  how schools can foster, 68–71,
    126–29, 191–94

how teachers can assist
in children in social
interaction, 192
how the money focus
undermines, 68–71
jigsaw classroom
arrangements, 151–52
measuring children's skills in,
191–94
"other-mindedness," 127
teaching one another, 70–7,
128
college educations, emphasis on
money and financial benefits
of, 35–37
compliance and obedience,
45–46
costs of focusing only on,
71–74
difference from engagement,
72–74, 157
and executive function
(control), 45–46, 71–74
conversations, 138–46,
189–91
about topics that matter to
children, 145
as core element of a school
designed to promote
well-being and happiness,
138–46
and engagement, 105–6
importance for learning,
138–39, 177, 190
methods for encouraging in
the classroom, 142–46, 190
methods for measuring
conversational skills,
189–91
quiz model, 142

and research on children's
language experiences/
environments, 139–40, 177,
189–90
talking sticks, 145
teachers' lunchtime
discussions, 166–67
teachers' roles in children's
acquisition of conversational
skills, 144–45, 189–91
Cosgrove, Toby, 181
"Creating a Community of
Learners About Things
That Matter" (Brown),
104
Csikszentmihalyi, Mihaly,
99–100
"The Curb in the Sky"
(Thurber), 142
curiosity, nurturing, 113–16,
153–55
as core element of a school
designed to promote
well-being and happiness,
153–55
fostering the disposition of
investigation, 153–55
fragility of children's natural
curiosity, 113–14
learning to form a question,
116, 154, 188
and the love of learning,
113–14
measuring a child's disposition
to inquire/ask questions,
187–88
in science education, 114–16,
154, 188
curriculum design and
developmental science, 42

de Blasio, Bill, 4
The Death and Life of the Great American School (Ravitch), 32–33
developmental psychology
  and curriculum design, 42
  Erikson's psychosocial states of human development, 107–8
  Maslow's hierarchy of needs, 86–87
  Piaget and research on children's reasoning, 118
  studies of how children learn collaborative skills, 193–94
Dewey, John, 20–22, 25, 110
DIBELS (Dynamic Indicators of Basic Early Literary Skills), 55–60
Dickens, Charles, 41, 155
Duckworth, Angela, 100
Duncan, Arne, 28–29
Dweck, Carol, 78

Easterlin, Richard, 84–85
Edison Project, 33–34
Educating Esmé (Codell), 149
Eliot, Charles, 18, 21, 25, 35
Emanuel, Ezekiel, 171
engagement (immersion in a meaningful activity), 72–74, 96–106, 157–59, 194–95
  absorption and "stickiness," 100
  and agency (self-efficacy), 74, 103
  as component of happiness, 93, 96–97
  as core element of a school designed to promote well-being and happiness, 157–59

as critical to success, 74, 100
difference from compliance, 72–74, 157
examples of, 73–74, 97–106, 198
and "flow," 99
how schools can allow opportunities for, 96–106, 157–59
measuring children's levels of, 194–95
and negentropy, 99–100
rewards of, 99–100
and teaching reading, 98–99
Erikson, Erik, 107–8
Estonia, 29
executive function (executive control), 71–74
  and agency, 45, 74
  and compliance, 45–46, 71–74
  self-discipline as predictor of achievement, 100
  three aspects, 71–72

Faraday, Michael, 25
Finland, 29, 137, 179–80
First Amendment, conversations about, 105–6
Fitoussi, Jean-Paul, 94
Flesch, Rudolph, 52–53
Freud, Sigmund, 192
Friedman, Thomas L., 31–32, 106–7
Fryer, Roland, 67

Gawande, Atul, 180
Gilbert, Daniel, 93
Green, David, 64
"grit" (purpose, effort, and engagement), 100

Groopman, Jerome, 180
group work, 70–71, 128, 151–53
    See also collaboration,
    cooperation, and getting
    along with other people

Hanson, Lee, 111
happiness
    assessments of children's
        well-being and, 195–96
    correlation between childhood
        happiness and well-being
        in adulthood, 93, 94
    as indicator of national
        well-being, 94
    momentary pleasures vs more
        enduring happiness, 92–93
    and money/wealth, 83–87,
        90–91
    research on components of,
        93–94
    and schools' neglect/disregard
        of children's daily well-
        being, 5–6, 136–37
happiness as a goal of education,
    8, 89–133
    building a pleasant physical
        and social environment,
        137
    conditions for meeting the
        goals, 161–69
    core elements of a school
        designed to promote
        well-being and happiness,
        132–33, 135–69
    core goals, 132–33, 135–61
    eight dispositions children can
        acquire in school, 96–133
    teachers' happiness, 165–69
Hard Times (Dickens), 41

Hart, Leo, 111
Harvard Educational Review,
    172
Hausman, Hannah, 110
Hawking, Stephen, 198
Hoddings, Nel, 93
Holt, John, 21, 60
Horace's Compromise (Sizer),
    163
hospitals, comparison between
    schools and, 180–82
Huxley, Thomas, 25

immersion. See engagement
    (immersion in a meaningful
    activity)
implicit learning, 58
inquiry
    learning to form a question,
        116, 154, 188
    measuring a child's disposition
        to inquire, 187–88
    See also curiosity, nurturing
investigation, fostering
    disposition of, 153–55.
    See also curiosity, nurturing
IQ (Intelligence Quotient) tests,
    56, 172–73

James, Henry, 18
James, William, 18
Jensen, Arthur, 172–73

Kahneman, Daniel, 117
Kelley, Laura, 75–76
kindness. See collaboration,
    cooperation, and getting
    along with other people
Klein, Joel, 67
Kohl, Herb, 21, 60

language environments, 139–40, 177, 189–90. *See also* conversations

learning how to learn, 123, 124–25. *See also* teaching oneself new things (ability to learn on one's own)

Lepper, Mark, 64

Lippman, Laura, 148

literacy. *See* reading/literacy, alternative measures for evaluating

Littky, Dennis, 162

love of learning
Carnegie's, 11–15, 37
and nurturing of curiosity, 113–14

Mann, Horace, 35

Many Moons (Thurber), 195

Maslow, Abraham, 86–87

Massachusetts anti-bullying legislation, 68, 163–64

mastery and the sense of accomplishment, 93, 121–23
and agency, 123
how schools can help children achieve, 121–23
and self-esteem, 122–23
and well-being/happiness, 93, 122

math education, 47, 60–66, 110
and testing, 184
views about goals of (practical purposes/for college admission), 62–66

Mead, Rebecca, 129–30

measuring essential abilities and dispositions (alternatives to tests), 179–96
collaboration skills, 191–94
conversational skills, 189–91
the disposition to inquire/ask questions, 187–88
engagement and immersion levels, 194–95
flexible thinking and use of evidence, 188–89
and how hospitals evaluate performance, 180–82
periodic samples gathered via videotaped data, 184–86, 192–93, 194–95
reading ability/literacy, 186–87
well-being, 195–96

media/journalism
focus on financial benefits of college education, 35–36
role in promoting education as means to wealth, 31–32

metacognition (thinking about one's own learning/thinking), 123, 125

Mismeasuring Our Lives (Stiglitz, Sen, and Fitoussi), 94

A Modest Proposal (Swift), 4–5

money/wealth as driving force behind education, 1–9, 22–38, 39–80, 81–87
and business involvements in schools, 32–34, 43
damaging effects on learning/schools, 6–7, 22–38, 39–80, 81–87
and the effects of poverty on learning, 82–83, 139, 177, 190

emphasis on financial value of college education, 35–37

journalists' role in promoting, 31–32

money vs happiness, 83–87, 90–91

Nation at Risk report on competitive economic threat of failing schools, 25–27

NCLB and Race to the Top educational agendas, 27–30, 42

and shifts of mid-nineteenth century and early-twentieth century American education, 15–22

and two-tiered visions of education, 6–7, 22

Morgan, Frank, 61–62, 66

Mustache (student film), 102–3

Nasaw, David, 14

A Nation at Risk (1983 U.S. Department of Education report), 25–27

negentropy, 99–100

New York Times, 17–18, 19–20, 31–32, 34, 66–67

No Child Left Behind (NCLB), 27–28, 42

Oates, Joyce Carol, 147

Obama, Barack, 28

obedience. *See* compliance and obedience

Olweus, Dan, 69

"The One and Only Ivan" (Applegate), 143–44

performance motivation, 78

phonetics (phonics) and reading, 53–54, 57–58

Piaget, Jean, 118

play and recess, 75–76

positional wealth, 30

poverty
and children's language environments, 139, 190

and chronic stress, 82–83

effects on learning, 82–83, 139, 177, 190

Prince, Phoebe, 68

The Process of Education (Bruner), 124

Program for International Student Assessment (PISA), 29, 179–80

progressive education movement, early twentieth-century, 20–22

Dewey and, 20–22, 110

influence on later twentieth century educational reforms, 21–22

and vocational education/job training, 21–22

"project-based" learning, 21

purpose, sense of, 106–13, 155–57

and children's natural capacity for industry, 108–9, 157

as component of happiness, 93, 108

as core element of a school designed to promote well-being and happiness, 155–57

and feeling useful, 109–10, 155–57

purpose, sense of (*cont.*)
  how schools can help children
    build capacity for, 106–13
  natural variations in persons'
    levels of drive, 107
  opportunities for children to
    make choices and identify/
    work toward their own
    goals, 109
  sense of making a meaningful
    contribution, 108

Race to the Top
    (educational agenda),
    28–30, 42
Ravitch, Diane, 32–33
readers, becoming, 57–60,
    129–32, 146–50
  allowing children to read
    what they're interested in,
    78–79132
  and capacity for immersion/
    engagement, 98–99
  Carnegie's early reading,
    12–13
  as core element of a school
    designed to promote
    well-being and happiness,
    146–50
  as educational goal for all
    children, 129–32, 146–50
  as factor in becoming better
    thinkers, 119–20, 131, 148–49
  learning to read by reading,
    57–58, 149–50
reading, teaching of, 52–60
  Bush Administration's Reading
    First initiative, 53–54
  and DIBELS scores
    (diagnostic tool), 55–60

Flesch's phonetic method,
    52–53
learning to read by reading,
    57–58, 149–50
and meaningful conversations,
    143–44
money/test focus and
    schools' neglect of, 40, 41,
    55–60
observations of four
    elementary classrooms,
    54–55
phonetics (phonics), 53–54,
    57–58
providing time for reading,
    55, 57–58, 79, 112, 149–50,
    197–98
a reading corner/reading loft,
    112–13, 149
the "reading wars" and
    battles over best methods,
    52–58
sight method ("look, say"),
    52–53, 58
whole-language approach,
    53–54, 57–58
worksheets and isolated
    skills-building (mechanics
    of reading), 129–31, 149
reading/literacy, alternative
    measures for evaluating,
    186–87
  ability to identify names of
    authors, 187
  grammatical complexity of
    sentences, 187
  size of working vocabularies,
    187
Reagan, Ronald, 25–26
recess and play, 75–76

rewards and incentives, role of,
    64–67
  and cognitive dissonance
    theory, 64–66
  paying cash for learning/tests
    results, 66–67
  positive reinforcement, 168
risk-taking, 76–79, 197–98
rituals, meaningful, 137

Schmidt, Benno, 33
The School and Society (Dewey),
    21
school attendance, 83
school community, creating a
    sense of, 162
science education
  assessing scientific skills,
    188
  Dewey on, 25
  fostering habits of inquiry and
    investigation, 154
  learning to form a scientific
    question/seek an answer,
    116, 154, 188
  nurturing curiosity, 114–16
  and opportunities for
    engagement/immersion,
    158
  and risk-taking, 76–77
  Sputnik and Cold War–era
    space race, 24–25
self-actualization, 21, 87
self-discipline. See executive
    function (executive
    control)
self-esteem, 122–23
Seligman, Martin, 93
Sen, Amartya, 94
Shtulman, Andrew, 117

simplifying goals and making
    shorter checklists, 95–96,
    163–64, 169
Sizer, Ted, 163
Smith, Frank, 58
Snow, Catherine, 145, 149
Spargo, John, 16–17
Spencer, Herbert, 25
"spoonful-of-sugar" approach to
    education, 106
Sputnik, 24–25
Stiglitz, Joseph E., 94
stress
  and amount of value placed on
    wealth, 85
  effects of parents' stress on
    children, 165
  and effects of poverty on
    learning, 82–83
Swift, Jonathan, 4–5

teachers
  and collaboration/kindness,
    193–94
  comparison between doctors
    and, 180–81
  creating conditions for
    happiness of, 165–69
  and effects of schools' focus on
    standardized testing, 29–30,
    174–76, 182–83
  how the money/wealth
    focus discourages people
    from the profession, 5–6,
    36–37, 40
  importance of autonomy and
    freedom to make choices,
    165
  lunchtime conversations,
    166–67

teachers (*cont.*)
  reducing checklists and
    number of goals to achieve,
    163–64, 169
  risk-taking, 78–79, 197–98
  role in children's acquisition
    of conversational skills,
    144–45, 189–91
  roles in children's social
    interactions/acquisition of
    collaborative skills, 192,
    193–94
  Williams College students, 6,
    39–40, 46–47, 48–52
  See also reading, teaching of
teaching oneself new things
    (ability to learn on one's
    own), 123–26
  examples, 125–26
  how schools can give
    opportunities for, 123–26
  and learning how to learn, 123,
    124–25
tests (educational testing and
    the focus on test scores),
    172–84
  and cash incentives, 66–67
  charter schools, 24, 43
  consequences of academic
    competition/comparison for
    children, 29–31, 69–70
  considering the necessity
    for objective measures of
    learning, 180–83
  effects on teaching, 29–30,
    174–76, 182–83
  No Child Left Behind
    (NCLB), 27–28, 42
  Race to the Top agenda,
    29–30, 42

Ravitch and, 32–33
reading and DIBELS
    diagnostic tool, 55–60
  reasons for children's
    individual differences in,
    176–77
  and recess time, 75–76
  studies of what tests actually
    measure/predict, 176,
    177–79, 184–86
  what improved scores indicate
    (and three kinds of evidence
    required), 177–79
  See also measuring essential
    abilities and dispositions
    (alternatives to tests)
thoughtfulness (how to think),
    116–21
  allowing time for sustained
    thinking, 118–19, 120,
    194–95
  "critical thinking," 118
  factors in how well a child
    thinks, 119–20, 149
  and innate intelligence, 119,
    177
  measures of flexible thinking
    and use of evidence,
    188–89
  methods for enabling/teaching
    of, 120–21
  research on children's
    reasoning, 118
  and time spent reading,
    119–20, 149
  using evidence to guide
    decision-making, 117–18,
    120–21, 164–65
  what it means to be
    thoughtful, 120–21

Thurber, James, 142, 195
To Kill a Mockingird (Lee), 143
Tuskegee Normal and Industrial
    Institute, 18

University Elementary School
    (Chicago), 20
University of Chicago Laboratory
    School, 20
Up series (Apted films), 48–50
U.S. Department of Education
    A Nation at Risk, 25–27
    Race to the Top agenda,
    28–30
usefulness, sense of, 109–10,
    155–57. *See also* purpose,
    sense of

video data and educational
    assessment, 184–86,
    192–93, 194–95
vocational schools and vocational
    training, 19–20, 21–22
Vygotsky, Lev, 128

Weedpatch School (1930s
    Oklahoma), 110–11
Whittle, Chris, 33–34
whole-language approach to
    reading, 53–54, 57–58
*Why Johnny Can't Read, and
    What You Can Do About It*
    (Flesch), 52–53
Williams College, 6, 39–40,
    46–47, 48–52

ABOUT THE AUTHOR

Susan Engel is a developmental psychologist in the department of psychology at Williams College, where she is also the founder and director of the Williams Program in Teaching. She is the author of four previous books: *The Stories Children Tell: Making Sense of the Narratives of Childhood*, *Context Is Everything: The Nature of Memory*, *Real Kids: Making Meaning in Everyday Life*, and *Red Flags or Red Herrings? Predicting Who Your Child Will Become*. A contributor to the op-ed pages of the *New York Times*, Engel also wrote a column on teaching titled "Lessons" for the *Times* in 2006–7. She has made numerous appearances on radio and television, including *Good Morning America* and *Today*, as an expert on education and child-rearing. She lives in New Marlborough, Massachusetts.

Publishing in the Public Interest

Thank you for reading this book published by The New Press. The New Press is a nonprofit, public interest publisher. New Press books and authors play a crucial role in sparking conversations about the key political and social issues of our day.

We hope you enjoyed this book and that you will stay in touch with The New Press. Here are a few ways to stay up to date with our books, events, and the issues we cover:

- Sign up at www.thenewpress.com/subscribe to receive updates on New Press authors and issues and to be notified about local events
- Like us on Facebook: www.facebook.com/newpressbooks
- Follow us on Twitter: www.twitter.com/thenewpress

Please consider buying New Press books for yourself; for friends and family; or to donate to schools, libraries, community centers, prison libraries, and other organizations involved with the issues our authors write about.

The New Press is a 501(c)(3) nonprofit organization. You can also support our work with a tax-deductible gift by visiting www .thenewpress.com/donate.